THE RISEN LORRAINE
THE ETERNAL WORD

a study prepared for "THE COFFEEBREAK" Bible Class to celebrate its 24th year of systematic study of the Holy Scriptures with Dr. Frank J. DePolo

this study is available on audio and video tape and CD.
For information, write
COVENANT CHRISTIAN CHURCH,
P. O. Box 258,
Belle Vernon, PA 15012.

e-mail: depolo@dp.net

Dr. Frank J. DePolo

Copyright © 2003 by Dr. Frank J. DePolo

The Risen Lord and the Eternal Word
by Dr. Frank J. DePolo

Printed in the United States of America

ISBN 1-591609-85-2

All rights reserved. No part of this publication may be reproduced or transmitted in any form or by any means without written permission of the publisher.

Unless otherwise indicated, Bible quotations are taken from the King James Version, Copyright © 1973 by Thomas Nelson, Inc., and the American Standard Version, Copyright © 1901 by Thomas Nelson & Sons.

Xulon Press
www.XulonPress.com

Xulon Press books are available in bookstores everywhere, and on the Web at www.XulonPress.com.

This book is affectionately dedicated to
Dr. Dwaine E. Lee
President of Global Action International
my friend, colleague, and brother

CONTENTS

I. The Origin of Doctrine 11

II. Event Of The Ages 23

III. Contrasts Between The First & Last Adam 35

IV. Understanding the Value Of the Resurrection 51

V. The Power Of Life 61

VI. Fellowship and Communion With the Father 75

VII. The Hidden Manna 85

VIII. Peace: The Cessation of Againstness 97

IX. Understanding Sonship 109

X. Divine Purpose and Provision 123

XI. The Function of A Resurrected Life 137

XII. The Law Of Permanence 147

Final Word To The Study 155

A Word of Explanation

As you begin to read this book, you will immediately notice initials and numbers in the margin. The book was taught over a period of 38 weeks. Each one hour session was recorded and can be ordered from the ministry. The initials and number designate that particular tape/CD.

Cassette Tape: $5.00 each (includes S&H)

CD: $6.00 each (includes S&H)

Covenant Christian Church
P. O. Box 258
Belle Vernon, Pennsylvania 15012

It is our hope and prayer that this powerful teaching will be a blessing to you, your study group, cell group or Sunday School Class.

CHAPTER I

The Origin of Doctrine

Scripture's lesson: ACTS 1

(FD 290-1)

When we observe and then interact with the current situation as it presently exists among the Lord's people, it doesn't take long to realize the single largest and most important need. It would seem that the issue of preeminent importance is that of **LIFE**. Everything can be gathered up in that one fact. It governs all other issues and matters.

When all has been said and done in relation to Christ and His work . . . in relation to doctrine . . . in relation to the Christian life . . . in relation to the entire work of God, the point upon which everything rests and revolves . . . and that which determines its practical and abiding value, is **LIFE**. It is not, for example, soundness of doctrine that is something in itself the determining factor. It is not even the Scripture alone. It is not New Testament order in itself. It is not a matter of deeper or fuller truth, and it is not a matter of the work or the service of the Lord. Ultimately it is a matter of **LIFE**.

Please do not misunderstand. The list of things above are all important and indispensable. In fact, they may well all be the identifying characteristics and issues of **LIFE**. However, it is very possible for every one of them to be present *"without"* the **LIFE**, and therefore to be ineffective. It is possible to have good sound doctrine without **LIFE**. It is possible to have a comprehensive and thorough knowledge of the Scriptures without **LIFE**. It is possible to have excellent and systematic Bible teaching without **LIFE**. It is possible to have an abundance of revelation without life. It is possible to be walking in perfect New Testament order without **LIFE**. And it is possible to have a tremendous amount of Christian activity or work for the Lord . . . and for it all to be lacking in real effectiveness, because of a lack of **LIFE**.

The case that I am presenting is not one of offering a choice between the things. The **LIFE** will require these things. It will either accompany them or be accompanied by them. My point is that it is possible to have all of those aspects of things **WITHOUT LIFE**, and therefore for this entire effort to be lacking in Divine vitality, Divine energy, spiritual dynamic, abiding effectiveness and undying fruit.

If that is so, then it means that there are issues which precede these, and those matters must be established in **LIFE**. There is something which must come before all or any of the things mentioned above. There is that which is basic to a larger grasp of Scripture, to a fuller measure of truth, and to a great deal of Christian work and service. Something comes before all of that and that something must be established.

Two Pertinent Points

This raises two important points, which I should mention at this juncture. *Firstly*, that we may **place or arrange things the wrong way**, and by so doing come to a false position where we have a great deal which is not getting us to the place of real value and satisfaction to the Lord. It is here that we meet with the tremendous handicap of much teaching . . . when the teaching remains as just a teaching. It is possible to be mummified by teaching . . . to literally be wrapped up from tip to toe and be smothered by teaching. There are those who cannot breathe because of the amount of teaching they possess. That is truly a tragic condition.

These individuals are familiar with everything that has ever been written or spoken about sanctification, about the doctrine of the Holy Spirit, about the Church, about the second coming of Christ, and about many other aspects of truth.

It is very difficult to give such individuals any new light. They have read. They have listened. They have been to all the seminars and conferences. They have been in touch with all the specialized ministries and groups . . . and this entire thing has become a "dead weight" insomuch that it has really become a handicap instead of a help.

There is a very great peril in having these things without the **LIFE**. And perhaps it is there that the most drastic work has to be done . . . which is the work of **"undoing"** in order to **"do."** This is what I mean by "putting things the wrong way" and in so doing coming to a false position where we know it all and at the same time it is of very little (if any) effective value. It is a false position in that to know after that manner is in essence to put us outside of the realm of receiving newness and freshness.

Secondly, we must re-read out Bibles from a new specific viewpoint. Especially the New Testament. **What is that specific viewpoint?** It is not the theological viewpoint. It is not the doctrinal viewpoint. It is not the academic viewpoint . . . it is the **SPIRITUAL VIEWPOINT**! If the preeminent question is that of **LIFE**, and it is possible to have all these things — doctrine, truth, Bible knowledge, etc. — and yet be without the **LIFE**, then our approach to the Scriptures will have to be changed. Simply put, we will have to re-read our New Testament, not with a view to learning doctrine . . . not with a view to comprehending truth . . . and not with a view to knowing the Scriptures as such, but we shall have to read from the spiritual viewpoint.

How Do We Read Our Bibles?

Our approach to the New Testament can be in two ways. **First**, it can be from what we may call **"the cumulative viewpoint."** That is, as we now have the completed writings of the New Testament, we may approach it as a completed whole. We believe that God has nothing to add to it . . . though He may have much more to reveal from it. But so far as the Book is concerned, it is final, it is complete. Therefore, we may approach it in its completeness. We may take a subject or a theme, and with the whole Book in our hand piece that subject or that theme together. It will be touched upon here and there and there throughout the entire Book. And as we gather up those pieces, those fragments, those touches, and put them together, we form them into a system of truth. We systematize the Divine revelation by gathering up its scattered fragments and bringing them together. We make of them a whole . . . so far as we can see or determine.

We may take subjects up, for example, like the atonement, justification by faith, reconciliation, and a multitude of other themes and subjects, and collect what is said about them from the various parts of the whole cumulative record, and put them into an order and they, in turn, become a system of doctrine. This is usually called Systematic Theology. We can approach the New Testament, or the whole Bible, in that way . . . from what we call the cumulative viewpoint. That is one way.

Secondly, we can approach it from the personal and experimental perspective of the writers and of the people to whom they wrote. Simply put, we may move with the apostles in the practical side of their life which led to and called for the doctrine. That is an altogether different way of approach. If you think about it, you will be able to determine which is the academic, the theological, the doctrinal . . . and which is the **living** . . . according as you meet with it. And the meaning of what was said earlier about having things improperly arranged and thus leading to a false position will become very clear to you. The big question – and it is an open question – is whether the New Testament was intended to be systematized as to its teaching at all.

I wonder, for instance, what Paul would think were he to come back today and browse the many books, booklets, studies and commentaries upon his letters. I wonder what he would think of the many doctrines and theology that men have made of the things which he said in a moment of inspiration and need. **I personally think** he would look at it with blank amazement, and say, *"How did they get all of that out of what I really said?"* I am not sure he would even recognize his own teachings today. I am very sure that he would be very doubtful that it was the right interpretation of what he said.

I simply raise that as a question, and yet include it as something upon which to reflect. Does not a **systematizing of truth** result in limitation . . . in a hard and fast mold which breathes death? The New Testament themes are far, far too big for our molds. You cannot systematize **THE CROSS** of our Lord Jesus . . . you can only go on your knees and worship, conscious that you see something far beyond your power to fully grasp. However, when you enclose or box in a system of truth, you immediately reduce it from its divine and eternal dimensions, and rob it of its power. In that measure, you have brought it into a realm of death. The Person of Christ, the resurrection of Christ, or any one of the great themes of the New Testament . . . when you so wonderfully bring together all the many fragments and organize them and then place them into a manual or a textbook . . . you have in all reality **KILLED THE THING**.

I understand that it may be very helpful and useful to know what the Bible teaches about various things. I am not saying that it is wrong to know that, to search out and to follow through, so as to know everything that the Word of God has to say upon any subject. But I am saying that it is a question as to whether the New Testament was intended to be systematized as doctrine or theology.

We must always see to it that we leave enough room for God. When you say, or any group of people say (be it a local church or a denomination), *"now that is the teaching on that subject, and you must accept that, you must conform to that,"* you have systematized things and created a mold into which you are trying to force people. Sooner or later you will find that it becomes a mold like the mold of the Law, to Judaistic legalism, which is bondage . . . which does not leave enough room for God.

The Jews had the Old Testament scriptures. They systematized those Scriptures, and so treated, they taught them thoroughly. They so thoroughly threshed out every fragment that one Rabbi drew up fifteen hundred added laws on the one law of the Sabbath. Now the Sabbath is governed by over fifteen hundred by-laws. You can understand what is meant when it is said that *"they bind heavy burdens and grievous to be borne and put them on men's shoulders."* And if they did that with every fragment of Scripture, no wonder it proved to be an impossible yoke. So thoroughly did they systematize things as to say in effect, *"Now this is the Law, analyzed and applied, and outside of this you must not move. Within this compass you must have your being. By this horizon you must be fixed and set."*

When the Lord Jesus came, and in Himself gave some interpretation to the Law . . . gave some light upon the Law, which did not fall within the compass of their system, **THERE WAS NO ROOM FOR HIM**. There was no room for God in His own Law. <u>**There must be room left for God!**</u>

How The Apostles Got Their Doctrine

(FD 290-2)

We must remember that the teaching of the Apostles was not hammered out in the classroom. It was not gleaned out of a Systematic Theology Class. Their teaching was hammered out in the practical occupation with situations and conditions in everyday life. They were in the work of the Lord, and in the work they are constantly coming up against situations of tremendous difficulty. They were being brought face to face with the biggest practical problems of human relationship with God . . . with human need. They were in the thick of these things . . . they were daily in the fire of persecutions and trials. And right there on the battlefield, right there in the thick of things, the doctrine was hammered out. To them, truth was not an academic thing . . . it was a practical thing. They found themselves in a situation which demanded some revelation from God the Father by the Holy Ghost. They were being forced to the issue that either God must give Divine revelation, Divine light, and Divine understanding in this situation or else their entire position would go to pieces. So the whole thing became an immensely practical question . . . and their light was **LIFE** . . . their doctrine was **LIVING**, because it had a practical and living background to it. There was a specific and definite occasion for every ounce of New Testament doctrine.

The letter to the Romans has been regarded as the most wonderful systematizing of truth, and it has been dealt with as a masterpiece of systematized doctrine. However, in its being written, it was not written as a treatise of truth or a declaration of doctrine. It was written as the outcome or result of the Apostle being brought face to face with the biggest issue he ever had to encounter. The entire position for Christianity was at stake. **What was it?** — The significance of Christ risen! Everything was hanging on that. His virgin birth, His miraculous works, His tremendous teaching, His Gethsemane victory, His death on the Cross — all hung on the issue of the resurrection. So you do not go very far into the letter before you find that the great basic and all-inclusive statements are concerning **CHRIST RISEN**.

The Gospel of God concerning His Son, *"declared to be the Son of God with power according to the spirit of holiness by the resurrection of the dead"* (Romans 1:4). And if you follow through, you will find that Paul, while dealing with every other issue, hangs everything upon the resurrection of Christ and what it means.

My point is that the letter to the Romans was hammered out, we might say, on the mission field . . . not in a theological classroom. Paul was up against something powerful, and this revelation, this unveiling, came to rescue the Testimony, came to rescue Christianity in an hour of dire need and difficult pressure. It was a practical matter, not an academic one. Paul never went to his study (if he had one!) and sat down to write a treatise which has become known to us as the Letter to the Romans. He was in hand-to-hand combat with a real and terrible situation, and this letter was being drawn out of him . . . **and that is why it has so much life in it!**

The letter to the Galatians presents a similar position. It was called forth to meet a specific occasion. Every one of Paul's letters . . . ever bit of doctrine that he ever gave was to meet a specific situation or an actual position . . . , it was to address something that had arisen in his life. And so the revelation that he received was for a meeting of that need or the defusing of that particular situation. We get the entire result accumulatively, and then we put these things together into a system and thereafter impose it upon everyone and say, *"this is Christian doctrine."* What we really need is to be thrust into the situation that makes that light and truth a matter of rescuing us from either despair or destruction . . . and then the thing is more than doctrine, **IT IS LIFE!**

I think it is a fair question to ask as to whether or not Paul knew that his letters would become Holy Scripture, and for the next nineteen hundred years or so be analyzed, studied, dissected, resolved and arranged into an organized body of doctrine and theology. I don't really think Paul knew that was going to happen. What he did know was that situations had arisen which called for a statement of

Divine truth . . . that called for the mind of God to meet that situation. His perception may have gone beyond that because there are hints to the effect that he thought that after his departure they would have these writings to help them. But we may be quite sure that Paul never looked down nineteen hundred years (and more) and foresaw that these letters that he was writing were to become such a large part of the cannon of Scripture for the rest of the dispensation.

DO YOU UNDERSTAND WHAT IT IS THAT I AM SEEKING TO PRESS HOME? There are two ways of approaching the Word of God. There is the **"backward way"** of starting from the end and working to the foundation . . . of starting with a mass of data, of material, and approaching it as students, <u>**or**</u> there is the other method of starting alongside of the writers and those to whom they wrote in an experimental way, and being in sympathy with them in their need, of being in kinship with them in their situation, so that their position is our position in a spiritual way . . . and that we must have the truth or revelation that saved and delivered them to save and deliver us.

See what a difference there would have been. Here are all these volumes written by men who spend their entire life either in a study or in a classroom, or in both, simply taking the body of Scripture and bringing to bear upon it their analytical mind, and dealing with it in that way . . . until you become loaded and overloaded with a systematized presentation of truth. **BUT THERE IS NO EXPERIENCE . . . THERE IS NO HEART-CRY . . . THERE IS NO AGONY . . . THERE IS NO GETTING DOWN ALONGSIDE AN APOSTLE IN THE HOUR OF HIS HEARTBREAK, SEEING THAT UNLESS GOD REVEALS SOMETHING AT THIS TIME, THE WHOLE POSITION IS GOING TO CRUMBLE AND BREAKDOWN. SEEING THAT ALL WILL BE LOST!** The true way is the living way! The true way is the way of **LIFE!**

God never gives His heavenly revelation as something upon which our brains are to take hold of for purposes of dissecting and analyzing. God gives heavenly revelation to save us in an hour of desperate need. That is why He allows us to be led into situations which necessitate a new revelation. God's way is the practical way . . . not the academic way. The living way . . . not the way of an organized, orderly system.

Take some of the great things mentioned in Scripture: *"According to his purpose which he purposed in Christ before the world was . . . "* — the eternal purpose. And then, as part of that or subsidiary thereto: *"Foreordained, elected according to the foreknowledge of God, predestined."* The speculative mind leaps at things like that! These words are tremendous hints. They are things which carry vast ranges of Divine intention. They are suggestive of something. There are implications here. We must get the whole thing. Then we begin to work on **"the eternal purpose"** . . . on **"election"** . . . on **"predestination"** . . . on **"foreknowledge"** — things all beautifully arranged until all of this is wonderfully systematized and stereotyped, set, and fixed. Its beginning, its end, its entire range is beautifully set forth. **AND IN IT ALL WE HAVE FAILED TO SEE THAT EVERY FRAGMENT OF THAT IS OF THE GRACE OF GOD.** Foreordained? Predestined? Elected? — all is according to the grace of God. And what is academic so often takes worship out, takes life out, takes wonder out, takes awe out. You can present these things in a wonderful way as a great plan of the ages, without the heart being bowed under the tremendous impact of it . . . oh, the grace of God to me!

Systems of Truth Can Be Dangerous and Cruel

That is why it is necessary to come into truth in a living way, and not a mental way. That is why it is possible to have the entire system of truth, and yet not have life. There is a fascination about certain Bible truths. However, it carries with it this awful danger of missing a practical application and a practical challenge. **The Christ of God can never be stereotyped!** We behold some of the paradoxes of Scripture. *"Chosen in Him."* — yet never coming into that choice, except through the infinite grace of God, and only on the ground that you recognize that it is not merely sovereign, it is of grace. You and I will never come into God's eternal plan simply because God has chosen us to be in it. There is another side. We will only come into anything for which we have been chosen in Christ as we come to the place where in utter self-emptying, in utter brokenness, we recognize that this is the grace of God. We must not put too much upon predestinating . . . there is the other side — grace, grace, grace, and we have to recognize the grace of God before we can know anything about the foreordaining of God.

That is why systems of truth have become so cruel. It is simply because they are one-sided. You can over-emphasize any subject until it becomes icy, frigid, stern and cruel. Cruel in the sense that many people will be driven to desperation by their many questions as to that subject. Be it predestination, faith or Spirit-baptism. The whole thing has to be balanced with grace. And we will only come into the truth of it by grace.

I only use those subjects as illustrations. I am speaking about the danger of thinking in terms of Divine schemes, as though schemes were everything. They are not everything. There may be a plan . . . there may be a purpose . . . there may be a wonderfully ordered arrangement, with every detail set in place — but then that can also be very cold and lifeless. What we need is **LIFE**. Life is a basic thing. We will never come into the scheme or Divine plan, except by the way of life. And the plan will only have its realization in parts and as a whole on the basis of **LIFE** . . . on the basis of Divine life.

Final Word

All of this does not mean that there is no system of truth, or order of practice in the Word of God. There certainly is. There is a Divine order, a Divine plan. There is a heavenly system. But the question is **"how do we arrive at it?"** Do we arrive at it by mapping it all out? Do we arrive at it by gathering all the Scriptures together and arranging them into an organized whole as to the order? We might put it like this: **"Take the New Testament and notice the order of the Church in it. Then bring all the many scattered fragments about Church order together."** Of the result it can be said: **"Now we have the whole thing. Now we can homiletically and hermeneutically put it beautifully and arrange it in New Testament order. Now we can have all of our churches according to this order. Now we can get the people together and put this order upon them and say, this is New Testament order, you must conform to that! These are New Testament laws and regulations of governing the Church!"** Are you going to get into it in that way? If so, we are going to have death . . . while we have New Testament order. It is possible to have perfect New Testament order as to the letter, and have no life.

That may sound hard and cruel, but it is true. It is not that there is no order . . . there is! God is a God of order, and God does everything in a proper and ordered way. And He has His heavenly system into which we must come, but the question is: **"How are we coming into it?"** Are we coming into it from without, as a set order, or is it going to grow spontaneously and express itself on a basis of spiritual life? That is the only way in which it becomes a living expression of the Divine life. It has to express itself from within by a principle of Divine life. You cannot have assemblies of people upon which you impose a New Testament order. You have the gathering together of the Lord's people in a living way, under the absolute Headship of Christ and the government of the Holy Spirit . . . And then you will find that the Lord's order spontaneously comes forth. **THAT IS LIVING!**

Which of these two ways of approach will determine whether the thing is life or is not life? Just at that point we reach the great matter to which all of this leads. Part two will lead us forward.

CHAPTER II

The Event of the Ages

(FD 290-3)

We resume by observing that everything is bound up with the question of **"the place of Christ as living"** . . . that is, with the place of the risen living Lord. The Apostle Paul gives something of an extra element to the resurrection of Christ. It is very significant . . . to be somewhat technical for the moment . . . that when he speaks of the death and burial of Christ he used the Greek aorist tense. *"He was crucified, He died, He was buried."* In using that tense He meant that the thing was done. It is a completed act, it is something which is accomplished. But when he speaks of the resurrection, *"that Christ was raised,"* he now suddenly changes and uses the perfect tense. That is not evident to the causal reader of the Scriptures, but when you begin to study the Scriptures and come across that, it is tremendously impressive. In fact, it is almost startling. It means this: whereas he says that *"Christ was crucified"* — there is no doubt about that — *"Christ died"* — that was done, that was completed — and *"Christ was buried"* — it is a finished thing — *"He was raised."* By changing his tense, he gives this force to his words: **"Yes, but He was not only raised, He is now alive. He lives. His is living."** That is the added thing that he brings in with the change of the Greek tense.

Some may think that to be a small thing, but when you look at the significant change of tense in light of the place given to the risen Lord in the New Testament, you can immediately see that it carries a great deal more than just a grammatical change on a certain point in the narrative. It signifies not only was Christ raised, but that He is currently alive. It was upon that, you must understand, that Paul's entire life, as well as his teaching, hung. Not just upon the fact that Christ was raised. Lazarus was raised . . . ah, but Christ lives! There is something more about Christ's being raised. **He lives to die no more!** He is alive right now!

The Place of the Risen Lord as Living

That gives us the key to our next level of consideration . . . <u>**the place**</u> of the risen Lord, of Christ as living. It might be helpful to point out one further grammatical point in connection with the resurrection of the Lord Jesus. Paul does not use what we know as the "**active voice**," he uses the **"passive voice"** . . . that is, he does not say, *"Christ rose!"* That would be the active voice. He says, *"He was raised."* That is the passive voice. He was raised by the glory of the Father. So far as Christ was concerned, it was God the Father who intervened in raising Him from the dead. Christ was raised by a sovereign act of God the Father. This means that the Father was watching over the entire situation, and at a given point **(THE THIRD DAY!)** He broke in. God was involved in the resurrection of Christ. The Father committed Himself to the matter of raising Christ from the dead. Personally, I believe that was the message that the angel brought in Gethsemane that strengthened Him. I can hear the angel say, *"Master, the Father says there is going to be a third day!"* This gives further added emphasis, that the resurrection of the Lord Jesus is one which carries with it all the greatest factors: not just that He was raised, but that He now lives. Not simply that He rose, but that God the Father raised Him.

This leads us to see that for the Apostles Christianity and the Church were not a system of doctrine, or a system of orders and practice. For them Christianity and the Church were vitally connected to the living Christ. They both existed on the ground of Christ being alive, after having been crucified and buried. In fact, Christianity was the expression of Christ's being alive. The fact that Christ was alive was being expressed and the Church simply became the corporate vessel of that expression. Christianity and the Church had no existence outside the fact that Christ was alive. Neither entity could be anything in itself . . . only in Christ as living.

That is what I mean when I say that the pre-eminent, predominant issue is **LIFE**. It is not an abstraction, it is a Person. It is Christ living. So . . . the basic and all-important reality with the Apostles and the believers of those days was the risen Lord . . . and their living in union with Him. That which was basic to everything was <u>**Christ as alive**</u>, and their being alive together in total oneness with Him. We must see what that union or oneness was.

Out of this every other thing arose. All doctrine came out of the fact of Christ being alive, and believers being in union with Him. All Church order and practice came spontaneously out of that twofold fact: Christ alive . . . and believers livingly joined to Him. There was no other way in which to get doctrine or order . . . in a living way. That one fact which spread its power and significance over everything for them in those days was **THE RESURRECTION OF CHRIST**. As you study the Scriptures, you find it touching everything on every hand.

You must come to the New Testament with this purpose in mind . . . with this fact before you. We must be impressed with the significance of the resurrection of Christ in this startling way. As you read the first few chapters of Acts, you discover that all the preaching there was nothing more than the proclamation of the resurrection of Christ. If you have not done so, take the first few chapters of this book and underline every reference to the resurrection . . . you will be amazed. Then follow ***"resurrection"*** on through the New Testament, and see how many facets of the entire revelation it touches in a direct way. You will discover that resurrection affects everything . . . that it spreads itself over the entire Book.

Resurrection: The Governing Factor

(FD 290-4)

Suppose for a moment that we broadly survey the place that resurrection holds, as we recognize that nothing else is of any value or meaning apart from it. In saying that, I know I am making a bold statement, and yet it is true that **nothing else in the New Testament is of value and meaning apart from the resurrection of Christ.**

Take the Gospels. What do we have in them? To begin with, we have the teaching of Christ. That teaching is very largely in parabolic form. You will notice more often than not, in a preponderance of instances, when the Lord Jesus presented truth in the form of a parable, He would link it with the phrase, ***"the kingdom of heaven"*** or ***"the kingdom of God."*** He would say, ***"the kingdom of heaven is like unto . . . "*** and then give a teaching wrapped up in a parable. Most of His teaching was given in that form or format.

Here is the interesting thing. After His resurrection we come across the words: ***". . .to whom He also showed Himself alive after his passion [death] by many proofs, appearing unto them by the space of forty days, and <u>speaking the things concerning the kingdom of God</u>"*** (Acts 1:3). After His passion, alive, speaking the things concerning the kingdom of God! We do not know all that He spoke after His resurrection. In fact, I think we know very little of what He spoke during the forty days. We know the character of one unfolding that He gave from His conversation with the two men on the way to Emmaus. He ***"opened to them in all the Scriptures, from Moses and all the prophets, the things concerning Himself."*** (Luke 24). Shortly after that, when gathered with them, and the rest of the disciples, at Jerusalem, He opened their understanding. **What does it mean?**

The teaching concerning the kingdom of heaven, the kingdom of God, was in parabolic form. **Why?** — Because there was not yet the capacity for understanding truth in its naked form. The Lord Himself said that was why He spoke in parables. There was not the capacity for understanding, so He gave truth in illustrations or stories. The illustration would fasten itself upon their minds just as stories fasten themselves upon the minds of children today. When they are grown up, they still remember the stories . . . but then they come to the real meaning that the story was teaching. When we think with our mature capacity, we realize that it was not just a story, but that there was a truth being expounded. **We have to develop capacity.**

Because they were spiritual children, He told them truth in the form of parables. They did not have the capacity for spiritual understanding. The things concerning the Kingdom were wrapped up in stories and they did not understand them. **Now . . . after His resur-**

rection, He is the center of the Kingdom, and all the things of the Kingdom become clear to them on resurrection ground ... when He opens their understanding. I don't think I am pushing things too far to say that during the forty days, when He was speaking to them of the things concerning the Kingdom of God, that He was opening to their understanding new things which had been said earlier in parabolic form with a veil over them. That means that in the Gospels the teaching of the Lord Jesus was all prospective to the resurrection. **IT DEMANDED THE RESURRECTION FOR ITS UNDERSTANDING!** It was pointing toward the time when in resurrection life there would be capacity for understanding it. It is clear that they understood after the resurrection.

If you continue studying the works that Jesus did in the Gospels, you discover that He linked His works with the Kingdom. *"If I by the finger of God [the power of the Holy Spirit] cast out demons, then is the Kingdom come nigh unto you"* (Luke 11:20). Even though they did not understand, He was connecting His works with the Kingdom of God. Whether it was opening blind eyes or raising a dead person, it was all linked with the Kingdom. **It was all looking forward!** Every miracle had a meaning ... has a significance. Whatever the miracle was ... from the raising of Lazarus to the turning of water into wine, all the works had a deeper meaning. They were **"acted"** parables and not **"spoken"** parables. They were looking forward to the time of the resurrection when the veil of the flesh ... the veil of natural limitation would be removed, and there would be capacity for spiritual understanding.

The Rent Veil

The rending of the veil ... the flesh, which was standing between God and man, and causing limitation, has been broken through and another realm has been reached. A realm where everything is spiritual and of God, and without natural limitation. With the veil of earthly limitation, of incapacity, torn asunder, there is now ability to understand spiritual things. There is no doubt that as they came to understand parabolic teaching, they also came to understand parabolic act. They saw that these miracles were acted teaching with a hidden meaning and that they had a spiritual interpretation. Into this realm they were now entering. This was to characterize the **"greater works"**, in conjunction with Christ's going back to the Father.

Opening the eyes of the blind. Yes, physical healing is available and of God. However, there is something more here. Paul saw the risen, living Christ and at the same time the Lord said, **"unto whom I send thee to open their eyes, that they may turn from darkness to light . . . " (Acts 26:18).** That is entering into the spiritual meaning of John 9, where we have the man born blind receiving his sight. Paul came into the spiritual value of the **"greater works"** which were not in the merely physical or temporal, but now in the spiritual and eternal. That is a powerful thing concerning the Kingdom . . . to open the eyes of the blind. Jesus is bringing His teaching onto resurrection ground. He is bringing into the spiritual realm teaching which has been waiting for this new realm before they could grasp it.

Take the epochs in Christ's life as they are seen in the Gospels: His baptism . . . His transfiguration. Each of these had a spiritual meaning and significance. After His resurrection (on that ground), the Apostles entered into the meaning of these things. They did not understand at the time. How could they understand His baptism or His transfiguration? It is very clear that they did not understand — On the Mount of Transfiguration itself Peter missed the point entirely and failed to see the tremendous significance of what was happening. However, he saw the light later, and when he wrote his letter many years down the road of time, he could say: **". . . this voice we ourselves heard . . . when we were with Him in the holy mount." (2 Peter 1:18).** He came to an understanding of the significance of the event.

I am not touching upon the meaning of these things (the baptism or the transfiguration). I am simply pointing to a fact: **namely, that the Gospels contain in teaching, in works, in experience and in epochs a great mass of data which the disciples did not understand until they reached resurrection ground.** After the resurrection it says that He spoke to them of the things concerning the Kingdom of God . . . and from that time they entered into the spiritual meaning of what they had heard and seen and associated with but had never understood. <u>**Understanding needed resurrection**</u>**!** On resurrection ground, in fellowship with the risen

Lord, they began to enter into an understanding. In just a short time, another change will take place. What was beginning to dawn upon them was soon to be brought out into full light. As He speaks it is beginning to dawn upon them. I can imagine that during those forty days they often looked very amazed and probably said to one another: *"This is wonderful! We did not know it meant that. We did not see that in it."* It was like the dawn! **And then . . . when the Holy Spirit came and took up residence within them . . . it was full daylight!** From that time they went *"everywhere"* limited no longer by a partial, imperfect grasp of things. No longer limited by the old ignorance, by the old darkness. Now the Spirit worked with them! Now in full daylight they have a complete grasp of what took place during the days of His flesh . . . a grasp of the content of the Gospels. Tragically many still do not have that today! Why? — they are not living on resurrection ground and the Holy Spirit does not indwell their lives!

Divine Life. . .Divine Light

I have not covered that ground to just leave you there, but rather because now we can see the tremendous value and significance of this fact in application to ourselves. What is it that we have in view? What is it that I am after? For one thing, I am saying that **LIFE IN CHRIST IS A TREMENDOUS THING**. To what does that work out? What are the values of that? It is with all the values of that we will be concerned within the remainder of this study. However, I want to indicate, from the point just reached, the fact that **there is a resurrection-apprehension of Divine things**, which is an entirely different apprehension from all others. A resurrection-apprehension of Divine things is a living apprehension . . . not a mental or academic one, not as of a system of truth . . . but a living apprehension. There is a powerful difference between having a thing **"explained to us"**, and having it **"revealed to us"**.

Please do not misunderstand . . . **I am not saying** that you cannot get truth in a class or in a sermon. What you get will help you. You will often come away saying, *"Wow! I didn't know that. That was new. That was great!"* **What I am saying** is that you cannot get the full essential of it. You can get the basis of it, but there is something more that you may have. That is, to have the Lord in a living way, make that truth received a revelation to your heart with a tremendous result in your life. I want you to recognize that it is not enough to have truth grasped in your mind as truth. It may be truth on any one phase or subject. It may be the truth of the Cross. It may be the truth of the Church, the Body of Christ. It may be any other phase of truth and it may be perfectly true. And because you have believed it, because it has gripped your mind, you may share it with others . . . and yet even as you talk about it, something is still lacking. Do you understand that? Do you understand that truth as truth is not all that we need? **It is necessary for the Holy Spirit to reveal it to our hearts!** I cannot emphasize that enough. This truth has caused a revolution in my life. That is what I mean when I say that it is essential that we have a spiritual kinship with the Apostles in order to have the understanding and value of their doctrine. A kinship with them in their experience is essential. I don't mean that it must take the identical form, but the fact or the meaning of the experience must be the same.

We must come to the place where from a mental grasp of the truth, which is really truth, we are brought through to a living apprehension of it. From my own experience there came a time when even though I had the truth, and taught the truth . . . that something happened and that same truth came forth in me as though I had never had it before. (It was in May of 1980). I hardly recognized the same things, and yet they were. Some said, *"What has happened? You are not saying different things from what you have previously said, and yet there is a big difference. What is it?"*

The difference is bound up with a relationship with the living Christ. It is connected with Christ Himself becoming the life of the mind . . . the life of the life . . . the life of the understanding. By nature the understanding is darkened. But now the Risen Christ becomes a new life for the understanding, and the understanding is redeemed from darkness. **No one can explain that, and no one can represent that!** It is something that you can know. It is an abiding miracle. The greatest treasure that the Lord has given me with Himself, but as a distinct thing, though not apart from Himself, is an **OPENED HEAVEN.** What I mean by that is, whereas in times past all of my work was a matter of intense study and research . . .

with a tremendous amount of mental expenditure in preparing sermons and Bible studies, now (since May of 1980) the Lord has been giving the revelation of truth. He has been opening up, and opening up, and opening up. Now it is a living thing! However, that does not mean that I can dispense with the study and research of the Word. But now it is a different thing altogether. Please do not misunderstand — it **is not** a direct revelation of something apart from or added to the Word. It is the Holy Spirit opening up what is there. It is the opening up of that which no natural mind can grasp. That is resurrection life for the mind, and it makes truth living and not academic or merely technical. It is something which is of **LIFE**.

I believe that is what happened to the Apostles during the forty days between the resurrection and the ascension. It was forty days of transition from parables of the kingdom to the spiritual revelation of the kingdom, and it was bound up with Christ risen and their fellowship with Him. It was a transition from knowing Him after the flesh to knowing Him after the flesh no longer (knowing Him after the spirit). It was transition . . . because the full state did not come about until they entered into spiritual union with Him, which did not take place until Pentecost. It marks a change. It is a moving from one ground to another. *"He spoke to them concerning the kingdom of God."* Simply put, they came to a position where they now understood what He had been saying to them, and doing before them, during the more than three years of His sojourn with them when they did not understand anything. It is the principle of **"resurrection life in union with Christ"** which makes truth a living thing.

Earlier I said that out of resurrection union with Christ everything else of doctrine and order arose, and that the resurrection spread itself and its significance over everything for them. I touched the Gospels with reference to teaching and the many mighty works in the life of the Lord Jesus. The same holds true as to His Cross. We might call that an epoch, but having so many sides and phases and meaning the Cross was not understood, except on resurrection ground. We can see that on the road to Emmaus. It is very clear that they did not understand. *"Dost thou alone sojourn in Jerusalem and not know the things which are come to pass there in these days? And He said to them, What things? And they said unto*

Him, the things concerning Jesus of Nazareth . . . and how the chief priests and our rulers delivered Him up to be condemned to death, and crucified Him. But we hoped that it was He which should redeem Israel . . . " (Luke 24:18-21). How little of the Old Testament scriptures they had grasped! How little had they grasped His own repeated explanation: ***"The Son of Man shall be delivered up into the hands of men: and they shall kill Him, and the third day He shall be raised up" (Matthew 17:22-23).*** Again and again He had said things like that. When He said, ***"Behoved it not the Christ to suffer these things, and to enter into His glory?",*** the *"behoved it not"* surely carried them back to the Scriptures, indicating how needful it was for the Scriptures to have been fulfilled. **But they had not seen it! They had not grasped it!** But now, on resurrection ground, they saw the meaning of the Cross.

Resurrection: A Change

Resurrection ground is not merely a further historic demonstration meaning that, because now they see Him alive, they have the indisputable confirmation of the Scriptures. That is not the supreme significance of the fact. That is a part of it, but it is not all. The thing which became the spiritual essential for them was not only that they had seen Him alive as a historic fact, but that the Holy Ghost came and inwardly illuminated all that related to that fact. They received more than the fact . . . they had all related facts.

Are you grasping that? — Supposing we were in the place of those men after the crucifixion of Christ, and that then while yet filled with all our doubts, fears, and despair, He suddenly appeared in our midst. We saw Him and listened as He invited us to ***"handle me and see".*** He dispelled all the ground of questioning and doubt. He put it all away and convinced us of the historic fact that He was alive. That is a great thing, is it not? But then, suppose that in some **new** way, with a **new** capacity, by a **new** power, a **new** enablement and a **new** ability, we were able to see and understand, in relation to that fact, everything in the Scriptures. We see it! We understand it! Yet we know we could not have seen it, but for a gift given to us for seeing. We have seen not the fact alone . . . but the entire range of that fact as it touched this, and this and that. The Scriptures suddenly became alive to us in the light of that fact (the resurrection!), as we were given a spiritual ability to see, to understand. **THAT IS RESURRECTION LIFE!** That is the range of the resurrection of Christ for spiritual value. Understand that it is only one aspect of it . . . but it is a tremendous thing.

Final Word

To gather that all up, it means that He Who is the fact of resurrection, and with resurrection life, comes and takes up residence within. He then reveals, by His residence within, all that is related to Him and His resurrection, making it of practical value . . . making of it a working power in every part of our being. **What a tremendous thing the resurrection of Christ is!** Every part of our being is affected. The resurrection is a matter of life affecting every part of our being and reaching to the farthest bounds of our horizon.

It was out of that that Christianity grew. Christianity was that! **At the beginning, Christianity was the expression of Christ being alive**, and that expression was within believers. If you had said to those early believers, *"How do you know that He is alive?"* All they would have been able to say, as many today are only able to say, *"He is a living reality within me! He, in the meaning and value of resurrection, affects my entire being. He has changed the basis of my being. This life touches me at every point . . . it touches my mind, my heart, my will . . . it touches my spirit, my soul and my body. Christ is a reality in everything. He is my energy, my life."*

What is the Church? — the Church is simply the aggregate of that. It is the entire company of those people in whom the Risen Christ in the power of His risen life, dwells and expresses Himself. By that indwelling, and by that energy, He expresses Himself in a heavenly order. He brings about right relationships. He puts people in their right places of function and gives them their due measure in every part. **But it is the expression of something within.** Christ risen means that . . . and much more. In the final analysis, it is a matter of that basic relationship or union with Christ in His risen life coupled with His having a full opportunity for expressing Himself.

I realize what I am saying is so different from the ideas of **"organized Christianity"**. I am speaking about the **"living expression of**

Christ". What He needs . . . what we need . . . what the world needs is a living expression of Christ as now alive in the perfect tense — not only was He raised, but He lives! For Paul that perfect tense means, *"Yes, He was raised, and He lives. But even now He does not only live somewhere afar off, but He is here.* **For me to live is Christ!"** That is the perfect tense: **"Christ liveth in me!"** He is present, personal, within and related as alive. That is all we want, and that means a tremendous thing here on this earth.

CHAPTER III

Contrasts Between the First and Last Adam

Scripture Lesson: Acts 26:23
"How that Christ must suffer, and how that he first by the resurrection of the dead should proclaim light both to the people [of Israel] and to the Gentiles."

(FD 290-6)

I understand that passage to mean that Christ, in resurrection, was to be the first One to proclaim light. Simply put, the proclaiming of light was first with Christ on the ground of His resurrection ... that light came by the resurrection of Christ, and that He, being the first One raised, was to be first to proclaim that light.

Leaving that for a moment, let us look at Romans chapter five and verses twelve and seventeen through nineteen. *"Therefore, as through one man sin entered into the world, and death through sin; and so death passed unto all men, for that all sinned." "For if, by the trespass of the one, death reigned through the one; much more shall they that receive the abundance of grace and of the gift of righteousness reign in life through the One, even Jesus Christ. So then as through one trespass the judgment came unto all men to condemnation; even so through one act of righteousness the free gift came unto all men to justification of life."*

Christ Risen: Meaning and Values

The entire realm and range of Christ for experience in life and service is dependent entirely upon His risen life in us. The whole realm and range of Christ covers a lot of ground and includes many things. My purpose is to look at some of these things. Of one thing I am sure. Nothing is possible in an experimental way, only in so far as the risen life of Christ **dwells** and is **operative** within. I want to emphasize the word **"operative"**, for **it is possible for the life of the Lord to be in us . . . and yet for that life to be under arrest. It is possible for it to be checked, thwarted, hindered and held down so far as all the Divine possibilities, potentialities and purposes of its being there are concerned.**

That is why so many who are true children of God, undoubtedly born again, having received the gift of life, do not make progress. That is why they do not grow, develop and mature. That is why they never leave the **"infant stage"** of their spiritual lives. It is because the life which they have received has not been given the opportunity, the liberty or the means necessary for it to develop them according to all the Divine intention. So in this part of our study I am concerned not only with our being the children of God and having the Divine life within, but even more with the expression of that life, with the values and meaning of the risen life of the Lord . . . or of the Risen Lord Himself as dwelling within.

For that life to have its full expression and proceed in its development unto the attainment and realization of God's full plan and intention in us and through us, in life and in service, a fundamental necessity is **the recognition of what is basic to such a development**. I might say that resurrection union with Christ is basic, but that is only to make a statement which is inclusive of other things. I want us to understand what that really means. I want us to understand what **risen union with Christ** is.

To proceed in that purpose, I must return to very familiar ground . . . to very elementary ground to some. It will not do us any harm and yet it will be helpful to some. By the enablement of the Holy Spirit, I want to attempt to present to you what it means to be **led out of Adam into Christ**. Recall the familiar statement of the Apostle: *"As <u>in Adam</u> all die (all were dead), so <u>in Christ</u> all are made alive"*, or to abbreviate the words: *"In Adam . . . in Christ."* As an inclusive, and perhaps a conclusive thing, we know pretty well what that means. We can state it in the simple terms of salvation. Yet I feel that its meaning has to be grasped by all of us in a very much fuller and deeper way, with a clearer apprehension.

There are three phases of our spiritual history. These are: (1) in Adam by nature. (2) In Christ representatively. (3) In Christ vitally. Let's pursue these a little deeper.

In Adam: The Darkened Mind

As to the first of these, we know to a great extent what is meant by the phrase, **"in Adam by nature."** Of course I am speaking of Adam after the fall . . . of *"fallen Adam"*. He is a type. The terrible thing which has happened in his spiritual history has affected his entire being. It has affected him in mind, in heart and in will . . . in spirit, in soul and in body. His mind has become darkened. A darkened mind is one which cannot grasp things beyond a certain point, which cannot grasp things beyond a certain range, and which fumbles even within its own range. It fumbles within its own compass, never reaching the ultimate ends.

In the Word the darkened mind is called *"ignorance"*. *"Their ignorant mind . . . "*. Simply put, an entire realm of knowledge is cut off from it. The spiritual realm, which is a vast realm in which eternal realities are, is closed to the ignorant and darkened mind. That mind has no capacity whatsoever in that realm. It has no access to that realm. In so far as the spirit realm is concerned, the darkened mind is totally incapacitated.

However that darkened and spiritually ignorant mind is not an inactive mind. Although it is represented as in death, it is not a death which is that of extinction. This mind of the fallen Adam is a very active mind. You only have to read the literature of this world, and especially in the range of philosophy, to see how active it is and how far it can go. All the literature of mysticism is but its seeking to pierce through that veil into that other realm. It seeks to grasp, possess and understand this spirit realm which is totally foreign and closed to that mind.

The darkened mind is a tremendously active mind. It is also a mind that seems to be very sure of itself. It is certain that it knows and understands that other realm. It argues, it affirms, it declares, it projects and frequently when a spiritual person encounters that natural mind, you come up against something very fierce. When you talk about the mind and about reason, you are only discussing one phase of the mind. We are very familiar with how far human reasoning goes. We are aware of the entire range of what is called rationalism . . . the action and activity of human reason. We have seen how it seeks to reduce everything to its level and attempts to govern by it.

This darkened mind is a powerful thing. It has created a world of its own. The mind of fallen Adam has created a world, in fact we might almost say a universe, and it is totally darkened and spiritually ignorant. It is within bounds beyond which it cannot go. Just beyond its bounds are the things which are eternal, true and ultimate. The natural mind cannot reach to that realm. This is the mind of the flesh . . . the mind of the natural man . . . the mind of fallen Adam.

The Desperately Wicked and Deceitful Heart

(FD 290-7)

The same has to be said about the heart . . . the entire realm of desire. And here, the desire, the heart, is something deeper than the passions or desires which lie on the surface. By that statement I mean that there are those of the more **"refined Adam"** who are not dominated and mastered by passions and evil designs, and who, on the face of it, would seem to be governed by the most noble and moral desires. But the heart of Adam is deeper than this, and who knows that heart? Not until there is a thwarting, a cutting across, a challenging, an obstructing, a resisting, is the discovery made that there is, after all, something personal in that desire. That there is a motive power back of the desire which is not the motive power of God . . . but of the flesh. The object of desire may seem to be very good, but **the thing which is governing desire is self . . . is personal . . . is of fallen Adam.**

Maybe I should dwell there a while longer to clarify that somewhat. Let us take what has already been said and apply it to the believer. In the work of the Lord it is possible – and often actual – for us, because we are persuaded with all of our heart that we are set upon the Lord's interests, the Lord's glory, to give ourselves to work for the Lord in a certain direction, by a certain means or instrumentality, in what we believe to be our calling for God. If anyone were to challenge the sincerity of our desire we would be hurt and feel very misunderstood. Then one day someone comes along who is better gifted and qualified for that work than we are. They come into the sphere of our work and others recognize their qualities and talents and put them into our place. We begin to feel that we are being forced out of our placement and someone else is being put in. **What is the reaction to that?** What happens? In nine cases out of ten there is jealously and hard feelings. This usually takes place inside. The personality changes. They become withdrawn and recluse, and often drop out of corporate fellowship and worship. Their explanation to inquiry is usually something like this: *"I think I just need a rest and maybe a move to another place of fellowship."*

What is the alternative to that? It is to get alone with the Lord and say: *"Now Lord, if You never put me into that, I am very glad to be out of it. If You did put me there, then I leave the whole matter with You. I am not going to put my hands on this matter. I refuse to touch it. If I am called by You to that task, if I am Your chosen vessel for that, then it is up to You to see that Your vessels fulfill their ministry and that nothing hinders them. I refuse to get upset, mad or sorry about it. I am going to leave the whole thing with You."*

That is exactly what Moses did. Do you remember how at the time when his position, along with that of Aaron, was challenged? It was said, *"Ye take too much upon you, seeing all the congregation are holy . . . " (Numbers 16:3)*, and Moses went to the Lord and, in effect, said: *"Now, Lord, it does not matter to me personally; I do not hold this thing myself, and I am not going to keep my hands on it and resist them. If you called me to this, then be assured that I am willing and obedient to you in it. If you do not want me in it, then I am perfectly willing to step aside. You always place the best possible in any task, and if You can get someone better than me, then I willingly step down. I only desire to see the work done. I only want Your will accomplished and Your desired end realized by the best possible means. If You have chosen me for this task, then You answer this accusation. You see to it, as the One with the mandate, that no one sets Your appointments aside. I leave it to You."* That is the alternative. There is no jealous feeling and no burning anger. That is what I mean by the Adam-heart and the new creation-heart. Remember that

the Adam-heart is always characterized by a personal element. Adam is always **"I"**. There is something deeper than what lies on the surface of desire. It is the motivating force of desire.

The Will: In Bondage

What is true in the case of the mind and the heart is also true in the case of the will. The Adam-will is a fallen will. It is a will in bondage. It is a captive will. It is captive to Satan through the flesh. It is in bondage to the flesh, though ultimately this bondage is to Satan. It is still a very active will. It is also a very strong will. When it is met and mastered it shows itself. There is always a battle to change it, and it is motivated by this deeper state.

So we have a spirit, soul and body, all now representing a kind of being which is alienated from God . . . darkened . . . and in bondage to Satan . . . and governed by deep-seated and deep-rooted elements of self. You can divide Adam into three parts, but not into water tight compartments. You can only divide the three by dotted lines (as it were) — Satan, sin, and flesh. That is Adam! These are three phases of him and they are all inter-related, distinct, and yet one.

Can you divide between Satan and sin? — Let us be careful on that point. There is something more powerful, more intelligent and more cunning than sin alone. Sin is not an abstract. Sin can never be a thing by itself. We talk about sin and sins, as though they were things which we could deal with in an isolated way. We speak of them as though they were things that we can get the best of . . . Now this is a sin, and that thing is a sin, and that other thing is a sin, and we are going to deal with these things piecemeal, as sins, and conquer them one by one. Begin and you will

discover that you are dealing with something more than sin. You are dealing with an artfulness, a cunning, a wit, an ingenuity, an intelligence or a personal spiritual power, which is more than a habit, more than a besetment, more than what we call a sin.

Sin is allied to personal intelligence . . . and they are allied to it. While they express themselves along certain defined lines which we call sin or sins, you can never put these two realms into water-tight compartments. The Lord Jesus in His cross not only dealt with sin or sins, He got back of or beyond sin, and the sins, and dealt with the forces of intelligence which were maintaining and energizing those sins.

The flesh! What is it? — It is the fallen nature of man, through which Satan by sin puts himself into action. He must have a means, a channel, an instrument for his self-expression, and the **"*flesh*"** is that which is in Adam allied to Satan and is always the instrument of Satan and of sin. It is always on the side of Satan. There is no difficulty for the flesh to yield itself to Satan, and be his instrument, his tool, his vessel or his channel. That is Adam! We by nature are in Adam. We by nature are in his way of thinking and desiring, with all its motive force. We by nature are one with Adam's will, nature and being. We by nature are all allied to Satan, separated from God.

In Christ: The Renewed Mind

(FD 290-8)

On the other hand, Christ is the last Adam. Here we begin on the same ground . . . mind, heart and will . . . spirit, soul and body. But what a difference! The mind! In Christ it is not darkened, but full of light. It is not alienated, but in perfect fellowship with God. It is not limited, but moving in the full range and realm of the ultimate realities . . . moving in the fulness of God's thought, of God's mind. This mind thinks as God thinks. It understands as God understands.

The mind of Christ is a vastly different kind of mind. These two minds are two separate worlds, two separate universes. They are always contrary to one another. The mind of the flesh is always opposed to the mind of the spirit. That, of course, is but another way of saying the mind of Adam as opposed to the mind of Christ . . . or the mind of the first Adam as contrary to the mind of the last Adam. **They are never in agreement.** When you have the one you have to repudiate the other. If you have the latter you are in conflict with the former.

The New Heart and the Surrendered Will

The same is true in the matter of the heart, as to the motive of desire. Christ is motivated by that which is totally selfless. There is no "self-principle" in Christ. He had accepted that basis of life here on earth, and was tested on that basis — and was perfected through testing on that basis — as to whether at any point, at any time, under any strain, He would act, move, choose or determine according to Himself. Whether as an independent and separate Being He would ever speak, act, move or choose as from Himself or in any way independently express Himself.

You get to the heart of everything in the case of the Lord Jesus when you recognize that the one question which constituted the testing ground of His life was: **WILL THIS MAN ACT ALONE, SPEAK ALONE, CHOSE ALONE, DECIDE ALONE OR MOVE ALONE?** – His answer was always, *"The son can do nothing of himself..."* *"The words that I speak unto you I speak not out from myself."* Every kind of appeal (as a test) was made to persuade Him to act or move on the impulse of the moment, or in response to an entreaty that seemed to promise success, or by an argument that appeared to be put forth with great wisdom... to act, move or speak as out from Himself. Whether it was understood by those who were the occasion of these temptations or not, this was clearly the design of the Devil as the instigator who was using them. At times the suggestion would be influenced by necessity of circumstances *("... son, they are out of wine ... ")* ... at other times by the promise of effectiveness in His service *("bow before me and I will give you the kingdoms of the world which have been delivered to me ... ")* ... and at other times by the scolding of the utter lack of wisdom for the way He was doing something, as when His disciples chided for seeming delay, saying, *"go up to Jerusalem and show thyself."*, and of His reply, *"I go not yet up to this feast ... "*. And then shortly after, *"when His brethren were gone up, He went up also ... "* The fact is that He would not go up at the persuasion of popular reason. He would not do this merely because it was what everybody else was doing, or because it was urged upon Him that, since everybody else was going to the Feast, He should go too. That ninety-nine people do a thing is no argument that the one hundredth should do it! We are not to be led by the appeals that decide the actions of the many — **"It is the popular thing to do! Everybody else is doing it!"** The surrendered will asks, **"Does my Father want me to do this?"** That is the question that must always rule our steps.

In the case of the Lord Jesus there was always a secret, subtle working to get Him to do the wrong thing . . . to get Him to act without inquiring of His Father . . . without direct leading from His Father. Always a temptation to cause Him to act in His individual capacity as though He were His own Master . . . as though He did not have to make an appeal elsewhere. **In Him there was none of that which was personal or independent.** I am not speaking merely of such things as sinfully personal, but simply of independent action taken with good motives and good intentions. All of this may be done, but apart from the positive word of the Father. That creates an independent thought, however good the motive may be.

The heart of our Lord Jesus Christ is governed by the anointing . . . is motivated by the anointing, and He always waits for the movement of the Holy Spirit in manifesting the anointing. Case in point: The delay in going to Bethany to see His friend Lazarus. That is Christ! Mind, heart and will reigned and harnessed to the thought, desire and will of the Father.

The Cross: Out of Adam and Into Christ

(FD 290-9)

How do we get <u>out of Adam</u> and <u>into Christ</u>? That presents our third point, which is our middle point. In Adam by nature . . . that is the first phase of our spiritual experience. In Christ representatively . . . the second phase. It is very difficult to adequately say what has to be said next without being misunderstood. There was an hour in the history of Christ when He virtually and representatively became the "first Adam". (Be careful how far you take that!) Christ did step into the place of fallen man. He was not fallen man. There was nothing of fallen man in Him, but He stepped into the place of fallen man. He stepped into the place of the first Adam, and took on Himself the sin, and the results of sin. At that moment all the power of hell pounced on Him to devour Him. This was their right to do so. Christ took on Himself all that related to the position of fallen Adam. He never, in His own being, became fallen Adam, but at a given moment He took on Himself all that we refer to as fallen Adam. And in that hour Adam collectively and corporately, all the members of Adam (ourselves included!) came representatively under God's judgment in its fullness and finality. That was the judgment upon fallen Adam and all that was bound up with him . . . sin, Satan and the flesh.

In that representative way we died. Adam was put aside, slain and buried, never in God's thought and acceptance to appear again. Christ in that capacity, as representative, died for us, and we died in Him. Not only were our sins put away, but we ourselves with all our good motives which cannot bear that eye of flame searching and knowing all about the jealousy behind them. In Christ it has all been put away . . . it is all gone! It has no standing in the presence of God from Calvary forward. The Adam mind set . . . the Adam mentality and outlook is gone. The Adam mind, heart and will all put away by the Cross of our Lord Jesus.

And then God raised Him from the dead . . . but He raised Him apart from old Adam and all that belonged or pertained to him . . . and so Christ becomes first in resurrection. In Him you have the new man, totally different from old Adam . . . in Him you have a man risen *"in Christ"*. We come to this last Adam by way of that representative union accepted by faith and registered in us by a work of the Holy Spirit. This is not just a theory. Many have seen the truth of what is called **"identification with Christ"** in death, burial, the doctrine of union with Christ, of being crucified with Christ, and they have viewed it only as an objective thing . . . they have believed it, accepted it, and proceeded to go on simply by the recognition of something and so they mentally or verbally accept it. It is as if a poster had been put up and they come by and read it, and say, *"I see that! I accept that! I believe that!"* And then they go on with their own life. They seem to think that because they have read the notice a change in them as taken place. Nothing of the kind! That is what I mean by **"doctrine without life"** . . . it is a systematizing and accepting of truth without a subjective internal working in them.

That representative union with Christ has to be registered in us by the Holy Spirit with the effect that the backbone of the old Adam has been broken . . . the sinew of Jacob's thigh is touched and withered, and he will walk with a crutch for the rest of his days as one who knows that his self-strength is gone. Something like that has to be done to make our representative union with Christ more than a theory or a doctrine. We have to be smitten at the very center of our **"Adam-strength"** with the Cross. That does not mean, however, that those things will never come up again, that we shall never see them again, or that we will never have any dealings with them again. It means that when they come up we can say, *"NO! I will have nothing to do with that! I know that God has touched that. That is forbidden ground!"* Many of you already know the truth of this in your heart. When jealousy comes up, for example, we can say, *"Woe is me if I go onto that ground! It will be disastrous for me if I allow that to come up; it will put me back on the other side of Calvary. Everything is bound up with my keeping off that ground if I am to go on with God!"*

If that were a living inner reality in the case of all the Lord's children, what tremendous differences it would make, and what relief there would be given to the people who have to do most of the **"spiritual nursing"** and who have to repeatedly tell the people what they should and should not do. They would never have to point out that a thing was wrong, if the Spirit of Him Who through the eternal Spirit offered up were known as dwelling within and saying, *"That was put away in Christ; you must not have anything to do with that!"* It makes all the difference! It is the Holy Spirit speaking in us and saying, *"You must not have anything to do with that!"* When you have entered into union with Christ through representative union, the representative union still has to be a practical thing and not just something doctrinal or theoretical. When you come into vital union with Christ you are on new ground . . . you are on **RESURRECTION GROUND** . . . you are on the ground of spiritual vantage where you are able to deal with Adam.

Let me put this into a very simple form through illustration: Supposing I have two men, one on my left hand and the other on my right hand. The man on my left hand is Adam. The Man on my right hand is Christ. By nature I am related to the man on my left. I am blood-kin with him. He and I are in vital union. It is not simply that we have a friendship or acquaintance, but we are one in our very life and nature. He goes wrong! He disappoints God. He listens to Satan and then enters into complicity with him. He works hand in hand with Satan in disobedience to God and acts contrary to God's known will. I am involved because of my relationship. God comes and makes His mind very clear to Adam in my presence, and I know quite well what God thinks about him, and the attitude He takes toward him . . . and what the result of his disobedience and unbelief is. He tells him that He had plans and purposes for him, but Adam has made it impossible for them to be realized. He says, *"I had a relationship with you, but now that relationship is broken. It can never be repaired."* He tells him, *"You must understand that from this time forward you are separated from Me in living fellowship, purpose and capacity. I will have nothing more to do with you."*

I hear that and realize that I am vitally related to Adam, and that this is the impasse to which I also am brought. I, too, am in that condition in mind, heart and will . . . in spirit, soul and body. I cry out to God and say, *"I am lost. I am undone. This thing has gotten into my very being, and I am part of it. I am in the same state as Adam. What is true of him is also true of me. What am I to do?"*

To my cry the answer of God is, *"I am going to provide a way by which you can be delivered. I bring One into your position, Who is neither in your state or position Himself, and He will voluntarily take the position and state on Himself, with the full consequences to their fullest limit. He will satisfy My desire to the fullest. You must recognize that by faith you have come into a relationship with Him. You have to repudiate this one to whom you are related [Adam], and you have to embrace this One [Christ] by faith. You must cling to Him."* **There is the issue!** — Will I remain in allegiance to Adam, or will I turn from Adam and lay hold of Christ, my Representative? If I do, then I am seen as moving, in that Representative, out of Adam. . .place, position and state. I am seen to pass, as by death, out of that realm, and then God steps in when I have gone down in death in that union, and with Christ raises me to walk in newness of life.

He says: *"You are now related to the risen One. But you have not seen the last of Adam, and you will see him often. He will always be prowling around. He is going to try to get you back. He will constantly try to influence you to his way of thinking. He will attempt to get you actuated by personal motives. He will seek to set self-will in motion. Your attitude must always be that you are finished with Adam and desire no interaction with him. Tell him you repudiate his mind, his will and his volition because you deliberately choose the mind of this other One."*

A Christ-like Attitude

So we have the two, and a choice has to be made. I am now, by the goodness and grace of God, in the advantaged position of being able to choose. At one time I could not do so, but now God has given me His Holy Spirit. He has brought the power of a new choice, and new determination, and by His enabling I can say yes . . .I chose Christ's mind and repudiate the mind of the flesh, the mind of Adam. I can now choose Christ's desires about things. I choose Christ's will and I repudiate Adam. I find myself constantly called upon to do that, and the fruit of obedience will be that more and more the choice will be spontaneous, and with deepening conviction from every fresh experience, I shall come to realize how infinitely perilous it is to delay on the matters.

Sometimes by a "slip" or by a "mistake", I shall be driven nearer to Christ and learn to be far more quick to repudiate that and choose this. Far more quick to say to Adam, *"NO!"*, and to this Man, *"YES!"* I am over on this side now, and I must keep on this side, and must never have any communication with Adam again. When he seeks to allure me, I say, *"NO. . .I AM FINISHED WITH YOU! I AM WITH GOD NOW IN THIS MATTER!"* Adam will argue and reason. He will attempt to persuade. He will offer prizes! He will make suggestions, reasonings and arguments. But I stand and say, *"NO!" "I am not coming back to you. I am not having anything to do with you!"*

That is the life into which we are energized by the Holy Spirit. Please understand that God never takes away our will, our mind or our heart. Some people expect God to come and do all their choosing for them. They expect Him to make all their decisions. He does not do that. He is developing a humanity. If we were spirits we might act differently. But we are not. God has created a being with a rational mind. The three-fold element of spirit, soul and body is still to be found...however, now not in Adam but in Christ. God is developing the Christ mind...how He thinks, how He judges, how He understands. When we see the Lord's mind we see how different it is from our own natural mind. Our own natural mind is so un-Christlike, so un-Godly, so far from the mind of Christ. **We must repudiate it!** This is spiritual understanding...this is the mind of Christ.

The same thing applies to our feelings and desires. They may lead us astray. We become a new creation in Christ by faith, however there is always the necessity of our standing with the Lord in what is of Himself. Passivity can be a ruinous thing. In all the values of Christ risen, there has to be a taking of that risen life for the equivalent need of the mind, heart, will...of the body, soul and spirit.

Final Word

There are values in Christ risen for our bodies now. His risen life can energize these bodies of ours **NOW!** Not, for the present, to change them into the likeness of His glorious body, but to quicken them for service. This risen life that is currently available for our bodies has to be deliberately appropriated, chosen and drawn upon. God has placed men and women in the body who have been given gifts that will make this risen life available to those who believe. The gospel says, *"these signs shall follow them that believe...they shall lay hands upon the sick and they shall recover..."* I often share that this way: *"These signs shall follow them that believe that these signs shall follow them..."*

It is useless for me, when I am feeling weak and ill, to say, *"Lord, I am just going to sit here and do nothing until You come and do something. You know where I am, and if You want to touch me, You can do it."* It does not work that way! He wants us to rise up in faith and **TAKE HOLD OF HIM!** *"The kingdom of heaven suffereth violence, and the violent take it by force ..." (Matthew 11:12).* He is saying, *"Lay hold of life. Take hold of Me as your life!"* The time has come to repudiate our conditions of weakness and frailty and lay hold of Christ for life. He causes us to co-operate with Himself on the basis of His risen life. All the values of Christ risen are found by our deliberate and definite taking hold of His risen life.

That is simply another way of saying, "repudiate Adam, whether it be in body, soul or spirit and stand in Christ for whatever your need may be. Is it for spirit? Is it for mind? Is it for heart? Is it for will? Is it for body? The one essential is to stand definitely in Christ for the situation. I come back to the point from which I started. The entire realm and range of Christ for experience is dependent upon His risen life in us, and our laying hold of it and standing upon it.

CHAPTER IV

Understanding the Value of the Resurrection

Scripture Lesson: Exodus 26:31-36; Matthew 27:45-51; Luke 3:21-22; Hebrews 6:19-20; 9:3, 12; 10:20; John 14:6

(FD 290-10)

That which is to form the subject of this portion of our study has to do with the question of our partaking, in a spiritual and living way, of the resources that are now at our disposal in Christ. Christ on resurrection ground and in resurrection life makes available to us all those secret resources of His own life while here on earth.

The triumph of His life — and indeed it was a triumph! — and the triumph of His Cross are to be accounted for by His access to secret resources upon which He was continually drawing. Those secret resources are now made available to us on the ground of His resurrection, and through living union with Him in a spiritual way as the risen Lord. Our task, at this time, is to discover what those resources were, and how they become available to us. We will only focus on one of these at this time, but it is the one out of which all the others flow, and with which all the others are vitally connected.

An Opened Heaven

Luke chapter three tells us that Jesus, having been baptized and praying, **the heaven was opened**, and it is with the meaning and value of the opened heaven that I want to share at this time.

If there is one thing above all others that the Word of God makes clear it is that **"heaven is closed to man in his unregenerate state"**.

You will find that to be the case wherever you look in the Word of God. The very elaborate provision made for man to draw near to God at all is itself a declaration that access to God cannot be taken for granted. It is not a thing available without very special provision. Associated with everything provided for man in the Old Testament is the warning: *"Stand back! This is for you only on very special grounds. There is no approach. There is no access."* I think it hardly needs laboring that the Word of God hammers out the fact that to man in his unregenerate state heaven is closed.

Heaven is not only a place to which we may go. So many people have but one idea of heaven as the place to which you go if you were good. We are all hoping to go there, but it is not in that particular sense that I am speaking of its being closed. The question of a closed or opened heaven is a much larger matter than that. Heaven is a realm of God. A realm of everything belonging to and related to God. It is the realm of God and His things. It is the realm of fellowship with God. . .the realm of communion with God. Everything of meaning and value and of necessity and blessing for man's spiritual good and eternal well-being is bound up with heaven.

That is not something future, it is something for the present. God's thought is not merely that we might go to heaven when we die, but that now we should know what life in heavenly union with Himself means; that what all the resources of heaven mean for our lives now on this earth, and that we should enjoy **NOW** every spiritual blessing in the heavenlies in Christ Jesus. Heaven is something vast for present enjoyment, for present experience. Of Zion, the Psalmist said: **"All my wellsprings are in thee."** That is now what the believer says of heaven, of Christ in heaven. That is heaven in present possession and present enjoyment. Actually, unless that is true now, before we leave this world, there is not much hope of our going to heaven when we die.

These things of eternal value and blessing for our well-being cannot be found in the world. Men have searched for them from the beginning of time. They have sought them the world over. . .and have not found them! They are in heaven and can only come to us through an opened way to heaven.

But all of this — and it is far more than I could ever describe or detail — all that heaven means of resource, value and blessing for time and for eternity is closed. . .is behind a closed door so far as unregenerate men and women are concerned. Tragically, many of them are even religious. One of the great snares which will keep multitudes out of heaven is religion. To be religious does not necessarily mean to have a heavenly life in union with the risen Lord.

We must see what this means in the light of an opened heaven. Clearly this is the significance of Christ's words to Nicodemus. He came to Christ seeking light about heavenly things. He wanted to apprehend heavenly things, he wanted to understand heavenly things. And the Lord Jesus very definitely and very deliberately said to him, in effect: *"Nicodemus, that door is closed to you.!"* Closed to Nicodemus? — he is a ruler of the Jews. He is a very religious man. He is a representative of God's chosen people. Yes, to him the Master clearly says: *"The door is closed to you, Nicodemus. There is no way through to you. If you want to enter into that realm, if you want to know and understand those things, if you want to come into those blessings, you must be born from above." "That which is born of the flesh is flesh, and that which is born of the spirit is spirit."* These two are totally different. They belong to two different realms. One belongs to earth, and the other belongs to heaven. . .and there is no passing from one to the other. You must be *"born"* into the kingdom of heavenly things.

The Veil of the Tabernacle

Turn to the letter to the Hebrews, bearing in mind the passages in our Scripture Lesson, all of which have reference to the veil. We know what relates to the veil from reading the book of Exodus. In the instructions given to Moses for the building of the Tabernacle, there were certain detailed directions for the erection of the veil to divide the Tabernacle into two compartments. The one in front of the veil was called the Holy Place, and the one behind the veil was called the Most Holy Place or the Holy of Holies.

In the Hebrew passages, we note that the Holy Place of the Tabernacle and the Most Holy Place are represented as "earth" and "heaven" respectively. It says that Christ, when He ascended, went into the Most Holy Place. He passed from the Holy Place to the Most Holy Place. The former is represented by His life here on earth. The latter is represented by His entering into heaven. In the Holy Place, there were the types of the things of God. In the Most Holy Place was God Himself. The veil hung between the two places, and death overtook anyone who dared to attempt to pass through that veil into the Most Holy Place were God was. . .unless bidden and by special provision. Concerning that place, God said that none was to enter in under the threat of death. Only once a year could the High Priest himself go in, and only then with the most precise governing rules and provision for his protection. Even concerning him, it was said that if he did not strictly, accurately and meticulously observe those governing provisions and rules, he, too, would die. . .even though he was a priest. **Why all these regulations and stipulations? — the veil declared that heaven was closed!** On the one side were the types of heavenly things. . .on the other side was God Himself.

Probing these Scriptures even further, we find that the **veil is said to be typical of Christ's flesh.** Because Christ has entered into the Most Holy Place, we are likewise bidden to enter *"through the veil, that is to say, His flesh."* Referring back to the Matthew passage, we see the veil torn asunder in the hour of the Cross. When He cried again with a loud voice, and yielded up His spirit, the veil of the Temple, typical of His flesh, was rent in two from the top to the bottom.

Let us take a backward look for a moment. Israel was chosen to maintain a representation of the things of God on the earth. Israel was chosen to be the custodian of the pattern of heavenly things. It was as though there was entrusted to this chosen people a model . . .which was to be exhibited for all to see. It was a model of something in heaven. And so Israel was called to maintain that pattern, that model of heavenly things intact on the earth. It was but a shadow or reflection of something else, and between the two there was a veil of flesh. That is, there was a human limitation between the pattern or types and the reality of God Himself.

In the Old Testament, the Day of Atonement was a suggestion of a fuller thought and intention of God. When one day in the year the High Priest, on the specified ground, went through the veil into the Most Holy Place, it was an intimation from God that He had a fuller or more complete thought, and that His thought was not fully and finally for exclusion, but for access. Human limitation was, so to speak, suspended for a moment, once a year when the veil was parted and the High Priest went through. . .although just for a moment, on certain grounds, and then it was closed again. Then the human limitation prevailed again, and for a whole year the reality was out of reach, and they were again bound with types, symbols and patterns.

When we turn to Christ we have the explanation of all of this. He came in the flesh. He took upon Himself a fleshly form. John's gospel opens with this statement: *"... the Word was made flesh and tabernacled among us ..."* In so coming in the flesh, he voluntarily accepted human limitation as the Son of Man. There was another side to Him, His essential nature, which still remained in union with heaven. He used that extraordinary word which sounds so much like a contradiction: *"The son of Man who is in heaven . . . " (John 3:13)* He said that, when talking to His disciples here on earth. Notice the present tense, *"is in heaven."* There is a side of Him, still in heaven, but now there is this other side, which manifested itself in flesh and has accepted human limitation as representing man. It is tremendously important for us to remember that as representative Man, as Son of Man, the Lord Jesus allowed Himself to become subject to our conditions of dependence upon God. That He put Himself in the same position as we, where the resource was not in Himself but in the Father. What is suggested or implied by His having taken flesh is human limitation. The veil is His flesh, and that veil, for man, means that heaven is closed unless something happens. It is that great **"something"** to which we come as the heart of our message.

All the sin which had occasioned the limitation of man in his relationship with God . . . all that had kept heaven closed to man, was dealt with and atoned for on the one great all-inclusive Day of Atonement, the day of His Cross, when as High Priest and Sacrifice together, He dealt with it all and entered into the full meaning of a closed heaven — for when He cried, *"Eli, Eli, lama sabachthani,"* did not that speak of a closed door or of a barrier in the way? Yes! He was forsaken by His Father in that hour when He bore our sin! He entered into the full realization of what it means to have heaven closed. You and I have never entered into the knowledge of what that means. God has wonderfully spared us that, while He offers to us the way of an opened heaven. May we not refuse it! When in His Cross He was made an offering and a sacrifice for sin, then in that hour the veil of His flesh was rent from top to bottom. The human limitation was torn asunder.

Resurrection Ground: New Life

(FD 290-11)

When Christ is raised from the dead, all that is gone. He still has flesh and bones, He still has a body, but the typical meaning of His being made in the likeness of sinful flesh has all been fulfilled and is now past. On resurrection ground He is released from every kind of human limitation. We follow Him and see how the limitations are gone. The **"time factor"** no longer counts. He is now truly in heaven while He is here. The first thing He said on His rising as He met Mary was: *"... touch me not; for I am not yet ascended to my Father; But go unto my brethren, and say to them, I ascend unto my Father and your Father, and my God, and your God" (John 20:17)*. The meaning of that saying is not readily apparent, but there is an immediate ascension. There is no division between heaven and earth now; the veil is gone. Heaven and earth are one for Him. On resurrection ground the heavens are opened. Those heavens that were closed in that hour when He cried out in despair are now opened.

All that was typified in His baptism. At the very commencement He set that forth in a typical way as the basis of everything. *". . .Jesus also having been baptized, and in praying, the heaven was opened . . . "* In His baptism He had, in type, gone down into death, been buried and raised again. And on resurrection ground the heaven was opened. There is a way through by the blood of His atonement. When He was raised the veil was removed, and the heavens were opened. All the patterns were gone, and the reality was entered into. While the veil remained, man was occupied with only the "patterns" of heavenly things.

Does it not strike you as significant and impressive, that when the veil was rent Israel was set aside. Israel had been brought in to maintain the testimony in **"types and symbols."** Christ had come and fulfilled all the types, and being the center of the types, the veil, that kept man from God and God from man, was now dealt with and the way opened. There was no longer any need for types, nor for one (Israel) to maintain them. **This is not the dispensation of the types . . . this is the dispensation of the reality!** This is the dispensation of a heavenly union with a risen Lord and of all that that means. <u>Our danger is of bringing back the types</u>! The types are gone. That is the whole message of the letter to the Hebrews. Christ is everything! The outward order of the Old Testament is set aside and now all that remains is Christ Himself. He is the Great High Priest; you no longer have priests on earth in the Old Testament sense. He is the Sacrifice; there is no longer any need for sacrifices in the Old Testament sense. He is the Temple; there is no longer any need for a temple in the Old Testament sense. He is the Church!

The Church: What it Is and Is Not

(FD 290-12)

What is the Church? — It is Christ living in union with His own. It is where two or three are gathered together in His name there He is in the midst. That is the Church. You do not build buildings and call them *"the Church."* You do not have organizations, institutions and denominations and call them *"the Church."* **The Church is not a building . . . it is a body!** You don't go to Church, you are the Church! Believers in living union with the risen Lord are the Church. This is the reality, not the type or pattern. His flesh, human limitation is gone. Now in union with Christ risen all human limitations are transcended. This is one of the wonders of Christ risen as a living reality. We are brought into a realm of capacities which are more than human capacities. Into a realm where, because of Christ in us we can now do what we could never do naturally. A realm where our relationships are new relationships . . . they are heavenly relationships. Our resources are new resources . . . they are in heaven.

That is why the Apostle wrote to the Corinthians and said that ***"God hath chosen the weak things, the foolish things, the things which are despised, and the things which are not, that He might*** *by them bring to naught the wise, the mighty and the things which are...* " Why did He appoint it so? — Because it is *"not by might, nor by power, but by My Spirit ... "* And also to show that there are powers, energies and abilities for His own which transcend all the greatest powers and abilities of this world.

That is the history of God's people, and that is where so many of His people go wrong. Men of the world look upon Christians and for the most part do not think much of them. They measure them by the standards of the world and determine that they are poor and without much knowledge. However, they are not able to measure spiritual and heavenly forces. They are unable to see what is happening when a few of those poor, weak, foolish and despised men and women get together and pray. They cannot see when they get together before God and are governed by the Holy Spirit that things are being moved around the universe and that the entire hierarchy of Satan is being stirred to its depths with the end result that the powers and principalities of the heavenlies are being pulled down by the greater power of heaven that is being brought into operation by faith. That is God's way and the world can never measure that! And that cannot be done by human wisdom, strength or ability at its greatest levels. God has chosen weak things for that! That is simply because weak things in their dependence are the best instruments ... are the best means of giving God an opportunity of showing that such works are not of any human sufficiency ... but are all of Himself.

Please take no comfort from the fact that God has chosen *"weak things and foolish things"* and say, "Well, I am weak and foolish and so it must be alright!" The point is ..., **are you bringing to naught the mighty and the wise?** It is not a case of resting on our weakness ... on our foolishness ... on our nothingness, and saying, *"That applies to me. That is all that matters!"* That is not all that matters. The thing which matters is that I, being a weak, foolish nobody, may know resurrection union with Christ in all His might and power ... and in that resurrection union with Him mighty spiritual things should be done through me. That is the positive side.

Heaven and earth are united in Christ risen. He is in heaven and yet He says, *"I am with you always ... "* We also have the statement: *"I go to the Father ... ,"* and at the same time the promise, *"I will take up my abode with you."* In the hour of his death, Stephen saw the heavens opened and the Son of Man standing at the right hand [side] of God, and yet that Son of Man by His Spirit was in Stephen, for Stephen is declared to have been a man full of the Holy Ghost. The Holy Spirit is called the Spirit of Christ. So Christ Who is in heaven is also living within . . . and heaven is also within . . . and heaven and earth are one in the risen Christ. Christ was seen in heaven by Saul of Tarsus on the way to Damascus, and yet He says to Saul: *"Why persecutest thou me?"* When Saul was persecuting believers the Lord Jesus clearly intimated that when he touched them, he touched Him. Heaven and earth are one in the risen Lord.

Typically this is represented by Jacob's ladder. Jacob stopped at a certain place and took stones and of them made a pillow. *"And he dreamed and behold a ladder set up on the earth and the top of it reached to heaven: and, behold, the angels of God ascending and descending on it: and, behold, the Lord stood above it . . . "* Heaven and earth had become united in that ladder. Bring that forth into the New Testament and notice the words of Jesus to Nathaniel: *"Afterward thou shalt see the heavens opened and the angels of God ascending and descending upon the Son of Man."* What is the meaning of this? — Simply that Christ is the Ladder. He has united heaven and earth in His risen Person. The heavens are opened because of the work of His Cross. The limitation is gone . . . the barrier has been removed . . . and in Christ we are joined or united with heaven.

Final Word

That means that with an opened heaven the Holy Spirit of anointing is given. In Him we come to share in Christ's anointing. The heavens were opened, and the Spirit descended and rested upon Him. That is the type. After His death, burial and resurrection the heavens were opened to Him, and the Spirit was given to Him without measure. From that time believers were baptized into Christ, and being baptized into Him, they came under His anointing. We need to always remember that our anointing is *"in Christ"* . . . it is under Christ as the Head upon Whom the anointing rests. We are baptized in one Spirit into one Body.

Thereafter everything is from God. All is directly of God now. No more types and no more intermediaries. The opened heaven gives us immediate access to God. Now . . . God is never very far away from us. Heaven and earth are united in Christ, and God is here, by His Spirit, in our hearts. He brings all the resources that He has. Now . . . we can know the Lord in a very personal and intimate way. Now . . . we may draw upon the Lord's resources in a personal and inner way. All that the Lord has is available to us inwardly. That is the meaning of an open heaven. All that followed in the life of Christ here on this earth, of secret resource, was indicative of this meaning of His baptism . . . that is, of an opened heaven.

We shall see more of those resources as we go on, but the opened heaven is a wonderful thing. Heaven is no longer closed when we are united with Christ on the ground of His atoning work, by which the veil has been moved and we are brought into God's very presence. We avail ourselves of, and give heed to, the exhortation of the Apostle: **"Let us draw near in full assurance of faith."** We have access through His blood. This is the new and living way which He has opened *for us* through the veil . . . that is to say, through His flesh. Ours now is an opened heaven, and all that the opened heaven means.

Chapter V

The Power of Life

Scripture Text: John 1: 4, 5:26, 6:57, 17:2;
1 John 5:11-13; Revelation 1:17-18

(FD 290-13)

These passages from the Gospel of John state explicitly that the Lord Jesus was in possession of a secret life by the will and gift of the Father. *"In him was life . . . " "As the Father hath life in Himself, even so gave he to the Son also to have life in himself." "As the living Father sent me, and I live because of the Father . . . "* Two statements are made here. One is the declared fact that He possessed this life: *"In him was life . . . " . . .* The Father gave Him to have life in Himself. The second fact is that the life given to Him was the basis of a relationship: *"I live because of the Father . . . "* The relationship was the relationship of life.

Our need at this time is to more fully understand the meaning and value of this life as connected with us with a relationship with Christ risen. In order to facilitate that understanding, we must return to these passages and allow ourselves to be led by them to a fuller unveiling of what this life really is.

This life to which the Lord Jesus referred was one of the distinguishing factors. It gave a special meaning to His presence on planet earth. By that I mean it marked a difference between Him and the rest of mankind. It made Him unique as a Man on this earth. There was not another man like Him. The thing that constituted a difference between Him and all other men was the possession of this life. It represented a difference which was recognized, felt and registered by others but, at the same time, could not be explained by them. Neither could it be defined nor understood. Many made attempts at explaining this difference, but they all seemed to miss the mark and their attempts always ended in total failure.

They looked in various directions for the explanation. They examined the realm of nature, but could find no explanation there of the problem which confronted them. Occasionally they would launch out into the realm of the supernatural and attempt to account for it on the ground of Satan: "He hath a devil . . . " "He casteth out demons by Beelzebub, the *prince of demons* . . . " However, with all of their many attempts, they were never able to get to the root of the matter. When I say they looked in the direction of nature and were completely foiled, I am thinking in particular of the bewilderment betrayed by their own reasoning: *"Whence hath this man these words, never having learned . . . "* That makes it clear that they had considered the question of education, and saw full well that education could not account for the difference. They looked to His upbringing, His training at home, His environment and His domestic life and exclaimed: *"Whence hath this man this wisdom, and these mighty works? Is not this the carpenter's son?"* His family was well known to them. The home He was born into and lived in were also known to them. There was nothing there that could account for His extraordinary and miraculous life.

It was even seen and noticed that there was something about Him that was even superior to the scribes: *"He spake as One having authority, and not as the scribes."* The difference was noticed but not understood. It was not natural. It could not be accounted for on any natural grounds of birth, up-bringing, home training or education. It was spiritual. When that is said, it becomes necessary to define what is meant. As we look for the explanation of this spiritual superiority which gave Him this distinctiveness, we discover that we have no alternative but to attribut it to the life which was in Him by the Spirit of God.

I want you to follow very closely the implications of that fact. The life that was in Him by the Spirit of God . . . that Divine life which is never separate or divorced from the Divine Person, and of which we do not speak as something in itself . . . energized every part of His being.

The Soul: Energized by Divine Life

(FD 290-14)

It energized **the mind**. Do you wonder at the mind of Christ? Well might we say, *"Where did He get His words of wisdom and power?"* Follow Him, listen to Him. Watch His ability go further than the wisest and the most intelligent of His opponents. They have their conferences, they plan their attacks, they muster their resources with wit, cunning and ingenuity to head Him into a trap . . . and He calmly goes on without as much as a moment's concern. To what do you attribute His ability? Will you say, *"He did it because He was God?"* While it is true that Christ is very God, yet in the days of His flesh He is seen living as a dependent Man, and not acting directly as God. So what is the answer: All of this superior wisdom, this ascendency of mind in the realm of knowledge, of understanding, of interpretation, of insight, of discernment and of perception is **the fruit of a mind energized by Divine life, by the Spirit of life.**

And the same Spirit of life can take the most ignorant and illiterate person today and cause wisdom to be found in them such as all the wise men of the world cannot resist. Men beheld the Apostles that they were ignorant and unlearned, but they could not question the reality of the wisdom by which they spoke. How do we explain that? It is the Spirit of life energizing the mind beyond natural ability. This, then, was the secret resource of the Lord Jesus Christ as Man. He possessed a life which others did not possess.

The same thing held true of **His heart**. What accounts for His infinite longsuffering, His amazing tenderness and His unspeakable compassion? How is His sympathy to be explained? If ever one's human patience could be exhausted, those disciples were capable of exhausting it. Had it all been merely on a natural level, at the end of more than three years of patient effort, patient forbearance, instruction, helpfulness, application and devotion to them . . . when every one of them broke down so ignominiously, and denied Him in spite of all that He had taught and said, surely there would have been a strong repudiation of them with powerful emotion: *"You are hopeless! I give up on you!"* — But not so with Christ! **"Having loved His own which were in the world He loved them unto the end** *[unto the uttermost]."* In every realm, except the realm of positive, deliberate, prejudiced resistance of Him and in what He represented, He showed the most infinite kindness and patience. But where that resistance was met with there was revealed in Him the wrath of God.

What was it that enabled His heart to go out to others? Look at the Scriptures again and watch Him in the midst of long and exacting labor. Work that was so demanding that there was not even time for Him and His disciples to take their necessary food. He bids them to come aside with Him and rest, and they depart for a quiet place privately by boat, only to find that when they arrive at their destination the crowds are awaiting Him. Do you hear an impatient outburst from Him? Do you hear Him telling them to send the crowds away? Do you hear Him asking to be left alone? **Not so!** *"Seeing the multitude He was moved with compassion,"* and He immediately begins His work again. What is it that keeps His heart so compassionate and so sympathetic? — It is the life of the Spirit energizing His heart unto compassion and sympathy in the midst of trial, testing, sorrow and pressure as no other ever had to endure.

You see the same characteristic manifested in the Apostles after His ascension. You only have to read the second letter to the Corinthians in light of what the first letter reveals to see the same grace at work in Paul.

Then we come to **the will**, and here we see the energizing of His will to do, and to keep on doing, the will of the Father. *"My Father worketh even until now, and I work" (John 5:17).* What a worker! Days of toil followed by nights of prayer. (We are going to be thoroughly ashamed of ourselves before we get much farther in this study!!!) We will begin to feel ourselves less than the dust as we look at this! **Remember that the same resource is available to us!** See the abandon of Christ. Never is there a thought of trying to spare Himself. Is He wearied? Yes, but a woman needs saving and so, forgetting Himself, He gathers up all His energies to concentrate on that woman's salvation. See the patience, the care, the application and the persistence that you discover in the fourth chapter of John's gospel. He is going to win. It is always like that with Him . . . willing, working and doing in fellowship with the Father. Never going beyond the Father, even in His doing. He was just as capable of ceasing from work as of working. His was a marvelously energized will to act or not to act, to speak or not to speak. It may take just as much Divine grace and strength sometimes to refrain from doing a thing as to do it. But **constraint** and **restraint** both have their explanation in the dictates of this life that is in Him.

Mind, heart, will; spirit, soul, body . . . all energized by this life. *"In Him was life . . . ,"* the Father gave to the Son to have life in Himself. It was on the basis of this Divine inner life that the Apostles were to be witnesses unto Him. Luke tells us at the very commencement of his narrative, in what is known as the Acts of the Apostles, that by the space of forty days He *"showed Himself alive by many proofs."* That word *"proofs"* is very strong and led to the addition of the word *"infallible"* in the Authorized Version. However, it is omitted from the Revised Version. Put all the emphasis and stress upon the word that is its due. You will not be guilty of exaggeration if you put all the emphasis possible upon it. When you do, you will be on your way to the true meaning of the forty days. **Why did He tarry for forty days after His resurrection?** — Of course, one reason is that He would have them to know without doubt that He was truly alive, that He had truly risen. He was giving them overwhelming proof of His resurrection.

So . . . the forty days were to establish the fact of His resurrection in their hearts and minds. The fortieth day was to mark His return to glory to receive the promise of the Father which was to make this that He had been demonstrating in their midst an inward reality for themselves. So . . . on the fiftieth day the Spirit came, and the purpose was fulfilled. It was in relation to the significance of this whole period that the Lord Jesus uttered the words recorded in the first chapter of Acts: *"Ye shall be witnesses unto me . . . " (1:8)* Witnesses are not, in the first place, individuals who talk. Witness is not a matter of words, but of power. *"Ye shall receive power after that the Holy Ghost is come upon you, and ye shall be witnesses unto me . . . "* What was the power? It was the power of the Holy Spirit. But what do we mean by that as regarding the effect or the outworking? It is the power of the Spirit of life!

The Church: Recipient of Divine Life

(FD 290-15)

On the Day of Pentecost that life which was in Him was deposited in them by and in the Holy Spirit. That is why the power of witness is not the power of words, it is the power of life. The secret of their witness lay in what they now were, rather in what they now spake. As a result of their being energized by the risen Lord words followed. Declarations were made, but it was not in itself a question of words or of utterance, but of the power in and back of all that was spoken. **"With great power gave the apostles witness . . . "** . . . not with many wonderful words, but with great power! What was the registration? It was the registration of life. Life was manifesting itself in them just as it had manifested itself in Him.

We again notice the feature of an energized mind. Have you noticed that at Pentecost the hearers were all amazed? What is amazement? It is mental defeat. Your mind is overpowered when you are amazed. You usually say something like: *"Well, I cannot explain that!"* Explanation is gone. Definition is ruled out. The mind is beaten. Here is an energized mind which defeats every attempt at explanation.

As with the minds so it also is with the hearts of these men. Listen to Peter as he speaks to the multitude, and notice the change of tone, the mingling of warning, of pleading and of entreaty. His heart is going out to them. You will find that was true of the Apostles from this time forward. One great characteristic of Paul was a heart energized by Divine life. It is a Divine energy, a Divine power, a Divine strength that is manifesting itself. Words are the vessels of something, but they are not things in themselves. These words are the vehicles of Divine energy and life. Is not this what the Lord Himself had said: **"The words that I speak unto you they are spirit and they are life" (John 6:63).** He was not just giving them words or ideas. There was something in what He was saying capable of making a tremendous change. **Spirit and life!** Creative . . . constructive . . . corrective . . . illuminating . . . empowering! You not only received a command or an instruction, but with it you received an energy to do what you could not otherwise do.

When the Word of God comes to our hearts, it is not just a

precept to be hung upon a wall and looked at . . . it is something which has in it the power that will energize us if we step out upon it. It is the Word of a King, and with the Word of a King there is power.

Do you now understand why I spent so much time in the first chapter pointing out the difference between New Testament truth systematized and the Word in life? Are you now able to see the danger of systematizing truth and thinking that when you have New Testament truth all orderly arranged, organized and pigeonholed, that you are going to have a New Testament condition prevailing? **Truth has to be entered into!** And it has to enter into us as LIFE if it is to produce its own order. It is life that is the primary thing, the Word, not the letter.

This and not His superiority as a Man among men was the distinguishing feature in Christ that made the difference. At least, let me say that this was one of the things . . . there were others. However, I am not dealing with them.

Life Ministry

(FD 290-16)

We come now to the second point . . . the ministry of life. In the fourth verse of the first chapter of John's gospel we read: *"In him was life, and the life was the light of men."* Note the words of the second half of the verse: *". . .the life was the light of men."* The life was the light! That is the ministry of life. In this connection it would be well to re-read that difficult passage from *Acts 26:22-23 - "Having therefore obtained the help that is from God, I stand unto this day testifying both to small and great, saying nothing but what the prophets and Moses did say should come; how that the Christ must suffer, and how that he first by the resurrection of the dead should proclaim light both to the people [Israel] and to the Gentiles."*

It is the closing statement that is so significant – *" . . . that he first by the resurrection of the dead should proclaim light . . . "* The first proclaimer of light was Christ, and the ground upon which He proclaimed light was resurrection. That is but a different way of expressing the second half of *John 1:4:* "*...the life was the* *light . . . "* The resurrection is the basis of light.

The point to be noted is that the **life** expresses itself in a certain way. It is seen to do so as **light**. If you continue through John's Gospel you will notice other things: the **life** will express itself in **liberty**. *"If the son shall make you free, ye shall be free indeed." (8:36)* But here the inclusive thought is that life has its own ministry, and that ministry is a matter of life. As was said earlier, ministry is not first in word, but is rather first a question of life through the Word. It is not doctrine. Ministry is not merely the imparting of truth, but the imparting of Christ through the truth. If the truth does not minister Christ then it is dead and without value or meaning. All truth, all doctrine and teaching must be a ministry of the living Christ . . . and not just a ministry of information about Him. The test of everything is as to how far it ministers Christ in a living way. When any portion of ministry has been concluded, the question is not as to whether it was interesting, edifying or instructive . . . but **do I now have a fuller measure of Christ because of it? Has Christ become available to me in a fuller measure because of that ministry? Am I confronted with the question of Christ as my life in a way that has not been so before?** — That, my friend, is the test of a ministry.

Christ may come to us through explanations, through definitions and through truth, but when these things remain something in themselves then it is not a true ministry. All must minister Christ, and that ministry is not just the ministry of certain individuals called **"ministers."** The entire Church is called into the ministry or the ministration of Christ. All the members are to minister Christ to one another, and when believers are gathered together it ought to mean life to all who are present. That meeting place should be a place of life. If it is, it will have all the symptoms of being alive. Vision, hearing, scenting, touching, speaking . . . etc. Going to that gathering of the Lord's people when tired or weary ought to result in your leaving saying, *"I feel refreshed and renewed!"* This is the life we have in the Son.

Do you see what ministry is? — Is it not a wonderful thing that when the Lord has a company of His children gathered together in Him and many of them arrive tired, discouraged, disheartened, worn out physically, spiritually baffled, mentally bruised and feeling that they have no resources with which to continue . . . that He is able, in the fellowship of the saints, to minister life . . . which is really a ministration of Christ . . . so that they go away refreshed and renewed. It is wonderful to come together for that alone, totally apart from expositions and sermons. **That is ministry!** When the Lord's people are really together in living relationship with Him as the risen One they do fulfill ministry, though perhaps in a large measure unconsciously. Others coming in and going away say things like: *"I didn't totally understand the teaching, but for some reason I feel so much better."* That is ministry and we are all in it together. Please don't think of ministry as something that is conducted from the platform alone. You are all in ministry, and it depends entirely upon whether the Lord's people are living upon the basis of the life as to how far they will fulfil ministry. **The life was the light!**

The Spiritual Conflict over Life

(FD 290-17)

Everyone in the Body of Christ is aware that there is a conflict, and that conflict relates to life. We arrive at that conclusion by the evident fact that the enemy's aim is to bring us down, to rob us of our life. **The heart of all spiritual conflict and challenge is Christ risen.** The historical fact was challenged. No sooner was Christ in the tomb than with an unusual spurt of memory as to things that He said, as though by the uncanny reminder of the devil, His enemies said: *"We remember that that deceiver said, while He was yet alive, After three days I will rise again" (Matthew 27:63).* And so they took precautions and asked for a guard and also asked to have the tomb sealed. The devil had already started his campaign to seeking to counter the resurrection . . . and he has never given it up! The resurrection was the one thing which disturbed and upset him whenever it was mentioned.

Not only was the historic fact challenged, the spiritual issue of that fact has been withstood even more through the ages. The means and methods of the enemy are innumerable and of an endless variety. It would be impossible to attempt to catalog the many methods or tactics of Satan to counter the truth of Christ risen as a spiritual fact in the lives of His people. I think we can note the borders of it. **On the one extremity** there is the naked assault of spiritual death; not through means or instrumentalities but nakedly as in the very atmosphere. You constantly are met by the spirit of death. It cannot be explained on any natural ground, even though you look everywhere for an explanation. You look to your own physical condition . . . you look to the physical condition of others . . . you look around you everywhere to find where it is that this thing of death has its source and you can't find it. Yet there it is. It is as real as anything can be. A power of spiritual death, a naked invasion of forces of death in the very atmosphere. It is suffocating, it presses upon mind and body, seeming to get right into your very being until you are unable to draw a line between yourself and this thing.

At the other extreme is beautifully dressed up truth. The Truth of God's Word marvelously arranged, ordered and presented with the most perfect diction, and yet as dead as Lazarus was before he was raised. Truth beautifully ordered, arranged and presented can be a deadly thing. It can delude people into thinking that it is living truth because it is beautiful, because it is true, because it is evangelical and because it is presented in a masterful way. — The true test is whether Christ risen is ministered to an increase of Himself in us. Not beautiful presentation of truth, but the measure of Christ in us in a living way.

Between these two extremes there are innumerable and endless varieties of death's challenges to the testimony of Christ risen. There is that **"false life"** which many call life because there is endless activity coupled with a lot of sensation, emotion and soulical stimulous, all couched in evangelical terminology. Yet all the while there is false life. Satan will contrive anything to lead away or keep away from, or to destroy the truth of Christ risen. These are our perils. These are the perils of a teaching ministry. It always has its peril of becoming a teaching, of resolving itself into a work of accumulating spiritual laws and principles without life. It must always keep life the primary and principle thrust.

This is why it is necessary for the Lord to **keep experience equal to teaching**. That insures keeping everything in life. To this end, He constantly takes us into depths and does not allow us to continue with Him without something in our experience which brings us up against **"living issues"**. The challenge and the conflict of life is a tremendous thing. We find it in every realm . . . spirit, soul and body. Quite often in the experience of His children a physical condition is due to a direct assault upon the body, and it cannot be explained merely on the ground that one does not "feel" good today. If we were just able to recognize that, we would not in that conflict just accept a natural explanation and leave the matter there. (I am not saying that we will never be ill in a natural way if we are energized by Divine life, but I do know from experience that assaults upon the body are very often an open attack by the enemy of our soul!) There are times when you feel ill without nature being accountable. The proof that this is so is that when you rise up in the name of the Lord Jesus and take Him as you **LIFE** you are better, and the issue has become a spiritual one and not merely a natural or physical one.

There is a wonderful redemption in Christ Jesus from those physical effects of the assault of spiritual death. **In such circumstances let us ask:** What is the nature of this? Does the Lord want me to accept this? There must be no sitting down and taking for granted that this is how it must be and so we must accept it! **WE ARE IN A BATTLE!** If the enemy can trap us along any of these lines he will . . . and the Lord loses in ministry when the enemy succeeds in this way. Remember . . . the resurrection of Christ completed the great victory over the spirits of death. Therefore, there is for us a heritage in resurrection and we must take it. Our inheritance in the resurrection of Christ is victory over the spirits of death.

Faith: The First Principle of Life

First, there is faith in the fact. This has been anticipated to some degree. We have already seen that **in Christ is life**, and that **it is a life which has conquered death**, and swallowed it up victoriously. Now the fact with which we must deal is that **that life is in Him for us**. That is the fact! It maybe objective to begin with, but it is a fact. In Christ there is life for me. Do I believe that?

With faith in the fact, the next issue is that of an active rather than a passive attitude toward it. This becomes a question of the condition of our spirit in relation to God's fact in Christ. Please understand at this point . . . I do not want to mislead you or to put you into a false position. I am not saying that your relationship to Christ risen is going to mean that you will never know weakness or meet with sickness. My point is that when we find ourselves in weakness or sickness or in any other way under an assault of spiritual death our spirit must be in an active state toward the Lord with regard to it. **DO NOT** go to bed and say, *"Well, I will stay here until I am better!"* You may find that the enemy does not let you get better very quickly, with the result that you stay there for a long time. Also, you may find that though you do come around sooner or later and get up and go on, yet you have gained nothing spiritually and there is no fruit for the Lord. If, therefore, you are forced to go to bed, go to bed positive in spirit toward God's fact. If you **must** pass through this experience, whether it be of a physical nature or of any other kind, enter into it and be found in it with your spirit toward God's fact in a positive way which says: *"Lord, I am only here until Your purpose is fulfilled. Then I expect a quickening. I stand for a quickening, and I wait for it. My spirit is open and reaching out to You that when the still small voice says it is time to get up I shall not wait for feelings which will help me, or for the whole thing to first pass away. But I shall say, The Lord's time has come and I put forth faith in this matter!"* In so doing you will find life entering in and with it the ability to do what you could not do apart from that life.

    It is really a question of the condition or attitude of our spirit. It will be found to be true that we do not get up until our spirit is quickened. If we do so apart from this, it will be a miserable existence . . . it will not be life. The point I want to emphasize is: **DO YOU STAND STRONG IN A WAY THAT ALLOWS FOR SUCH A QUICKENING?** You may not be able to pray, and the question asked is **not** *"are you praying?"* You may not be able to read the Word, and I am not saying you should be able to do so. We all know that are times when due to physical attack we are unable to pray or to read the Scriptures. But that does not necessarily mean that **IN SPIRIT** we cannot be holding on to God. Inarticulate maybe . . . yet holding on to God! Waiting for God, even though the mind is a blank and the feelings are dead . . . and God has seemingly left your universe . . . and the devil is saying that you are abandoned and that nothing but death awaits you. It is a case of faith being positively linked with God's fact with the spirit still toward God . . . not turning toward circumstances or our own condition, but toward God!

If you are unable to grasp that, or if you cannot follow that, at least grasp the principle. The principle is this: **FAITH IN GOD'S FACT MUST BE A CO-OPERATING FAITH AND NOT A PASSIVE FAITH.**

Second, we must have faith in a person and not in an abstract element. That is surely the challenge of John chapter eleven. The Bethany sisters went round and round in a circle on the question of death and resurrection. They were looking at the matter in the abstract. What had overtaken their brother was, to them, the inevitable fact of death. To them resurrection was a thing for the *"last day."* But all was changed when they were confronted with the statement: *"I am the resurrection and the life . . . "* That is not a time matter, not something confined to the *"last day."* That is a universal, timeless, present matter. *"I AM!"* That can mean **anything at any moment**. I end this portion with Revelation 1:17-18: *"I am . . . the Living One . . . "* May the Lord make this life to us. May He make it a real ministry of Himself.

CHAPTER VI

Fellowship and Communion with the Father

Scripture Text: John 5:19-20, 30; 16:13; Romans 8:2, 6

(FD 290-18)

These statements of the Lord Jesus from the fifth chapter of John's Gospel contain two or three elements. The **first** is that they constitute a clear and definite statement of what might be called **"a negative fact.**" *"I can do nothing . . . " "The Son can do nothing of himself!"* That is a very plain statement, but there are in that statement two inferences. One is that inasmuch as He is, at this very time of speaking, doing things, even as He had declared: *"My Father worketh even until now and I work . . . "* — and that is connected with the healing of this man as recorded in the first part of the chapter — and saying that none of this activity is from Him alone, then He must have another source of action and word. Another secret source is in operation. It is not the case that, because He can neither do or speak out of Himself, that He is therefore silent and inactive. The fact of His not being able to do or speak of Himself has not arrested utterance nor checked action . . . meaning that another secret source of expression is operating.

Secondly, these Scriptures reveal the positive statement that draws a contrast and marks a difference. The difference is between Himself and others. To get the force of that we can stress a certain part of the sentences: *"The Son can do nothing out from Himself . . . " "I can of myself do nothing . . . "* Here is One who is alone in this matter. Here is One who is unique. It is a statement which immediately draws a light between Himself and all the rest of mankind. **That which characterizes the natural man is the fact that he does speak and act out from himself.** It is characteristic of all men in their nature to do that, simply because their first fallen father did so in such a way as to involve all his progeny. This was the very essence of the Fall. Adam deliberately acted out of himself when God's clear and expressed will for him was that he should not do so. The Divine will was that he should speak and act out from God. He broke away from God as his source of thinking and acting and began to speak and act independently . . . out of himself. **THAT BROUGHT ABOUT THE FALL!** All men now think and act independently of God. It is the mark of the natural man. **But here is One Who does nothing after that principle.** It is a contrasting statement and shows God's mind about man. It also shows what God is seeking to do in all those who come into a living relationship with Him.

See how this works out in the chapter before us. **Because the Lord Jesus never thinks, speaks or acts out from Himself the result is life**: *"For as the Father raiseth the dead and quickeneth them, even so the Son also quickeneth whom he will" (v 21).* The result is life. You have a contrast presented in the chapter which opens with the healing of the man at the Pool of Bethesda. *"And a certain man was there, which had been thirty and eight years in his infirmity" (v 5).* The Lord Jesus healed him, and the Jews came to the man and said, *"It is the Sabbath"(v 10).* Later it is said: *"And for this cause did the Jews persecute Jesus, because he did these things on the Sabbath" (v 16).* Still another Scripture says: *"For this cause therefore the Jews sought the more to kill him, because he not only brake the Sabbath, but also called God his own Father, making himself equal with God" (v 18).*

First they persecuted Him because He did these things on the Sabbath, and then they sought to kill Him, because He broke the Sabbath and called God His Father. Can you not see the opposite action? There is a working of death. **Why?** Because they were thinking, reasoning, acting and speaking out from their own interpretation of the Law . . . instead of out of a Divine revelation of the Law. They had the Law, but they construed it according to their own judgment. They interpreted it according to their own natural mind . . . applied it according to their own natural will . . . and the result was death.

The Lord Jesus had a secret knowledge and understanding which they did not have. He was drawing upon that and **not upon** His own reasoning, **not upon** His own interpretation **or upon** the traditional grounds . . . **but upon** spiritual. That is why His activity was always in the direction of life. In this chapter you see the conflict between those who think, speak and act as *"out from themselves"* — even though it is in a religious way — and One who is not thinking, speaking or acting *"out from Himself"*, but in the Spirit. There is always conflict between these two sources, and the two effects or results are life and death.

What is the word upon which all of that hangs? – *"My Father worketh even until now, and I work."* The Sabbath Day! Yet, but how shall a man judge it? How shall he deal correctly with Scriptures regarding it? These Jews called God their Father, and did not know how they contradicted such a claim, nor did they know how their actions gave testimony that theirs was not a living faith in Him. When Jesus called the Father His Father: *"<u>My Father</u> worketh even until now. . . ,"* they sought to kill Him. But the Lord Jesus is working in life on the basis of a secret fellowship with the Father, by which He knows what the Father is doing, how He is doing it and when He is doing it. It is a secret source of fellowship and communion that is resulting in life. Without that there may be religious activity along with everything of tradition . . . and yet the result be death.

The Relationship of a Common Life

I want to pull all of this together and make a few definite statements. We can see that what is behind the life of the Lord Jesus is a secret fellowship and communion with the Father. <u>**The first thing**</u> which becomes very clear is that **it was a relationship of life by the Holy Spirit**. This particular relationship between the Lord Jesus as the Son of Man and the Father, as distinct from His relationship in essential oneness, deity and Godhead as the Son of God, was on a basis of a common life . . . on the basis of one life with the Father. That life was the secret of His fellowship and communion.

That is a simple statement which everyone should be able to grasp and it vitally affects us, for we find that after Calvary, when

He is resurrected from the dead, our relationship with the Father in Christ is on the basis of sharing a common life. ***"God hath given unto us eternal life, and this life is in His Son . . . "*** (1 John 5:11). That is the life which was, and is, in the Son, and we have it in Him. So then, as partakers together of the one life we have been brought into a relationship which is to work out in fellowship, in communion and in interaction. Everything issues from that.

I need not stay longer with this except to point out how many and varied are the things to which people fondly cling as a basis of true relationship with God. I fear that there are multitudes of Christians who honestly believe that they have a relationship with God, have an incorrect basis for that belief. The basis may be that they grew up in a Christian home. Or it may be that they have accepted the tenets of the Christian faith, or adhere to Christian principles. It may even be that they faithfully attend "their" church and daily read their Bible. They believe that their relationship with God is a good one and that all is well with them on these grounds. Unless I have sadly misread the New Testament, **the one and only true basis of a relationship with God is that of sharing God's Own life by its impartation to us in regeneration resulting in a new birth**. Simply put, it is the possessing of the very life of God Himself, which no one possesses by human nature. I know that hardly needs to be said, let alone stressed . . . but I do so as a way of explaining what I mean by the relationship between Christ, as Man, and the Father being the same as that into which we are brought by new birth. It is necessary to see that the relationship is that of **LIFE BY THE HOLY SPIRIT**, even as He said: ***"As the Father hath life in Himself, even so hath he given to the Son to have life in himself."*** It is a Divine impartation.

The Law of the Spirit of Life

(FD 290-19)

The second thing is that the relationship works itself out in life. Fundamentally it is a relationship of life, but it is a relationship which works itself out by life. If you quietly read through the life of the Lord Jesus, watching for indications of a government which does not lie on the surface, but which acts and reacts to what is seen on the surface, you will find much that makes it very clear that everything in His life is coming from another, secret source.

The times of His movements are governed times. They are not impulsive, they are governed. You cannot get away from the fact that these set, fixed times are not haphazard. Any time will not do for Him. A good case in point was His delay in coming to Bethany for His sick friend Lazarus. Just any time will not do for Him. He has to have the **"true time"** for everything. I have attempted to show that His life was largely governed by that principle. His watchword seemed to be: *"Mine hour . . . " "The hour is not yet . . . " "The hour is come . . . "* Very early in His public life His mother sought, by an appeal of need, to persuade Him to act in relation to the depleted wine supply. No appeal of circumstance, of need, of persuasion, of sentiment, of human affection, or of anything else of earth, man or nature could persuade Him. His ready reply was always, *"Mine hour is not yet come . . . "* However, that time came very quickly. The feast did not proceed much further before His hour came. It seems to almost follow immediately. There appears to have been just enough time for His mother to say to the servants, *"Whatsoever he saith unto you, do it . . . "*, and the hour had come. But the point is, if there is only the space of three minutes, He will wait for it. He will not anticipate it one minute early. **HIS TIMES ARE GOVERNED!** *"I go not yet up to this feast!"* Then when the others had gone up, He went up. What was the governing thing? *"Mine hour is not yet . . . "* Now His hour had evidently come. And it only took a little while. It may be but a few hours between *"My hour is not yet,"* and the arrival of the hour. There is something in the heavenly realm that pertains to our **"times."** The times are governing His acts, and His acts are the expression of set times.

With His words it is the same. He speaks not His Own words. He is counting upon the Father for the words all the time. He is receiving His words from a secret source. Times, acts, and words were all governed by the Father.

We are confronted with the question: **By what means did the Father govern?** How did the Father govern times, actions and words? To rearrange the question: How did Jesus know when the time had come, and what the words were, and what acts to perform?

I think the answer is simply by life. By the quickening of the Spirit . . . by the quickening of the life-giving Spirit. There is a law of the Spirit of Life in Christ.

We speak about **natural laws**. What are they? Take, for example, the natural law of nourishment. Provided that law is complied with and at the right time the body is given what it needs . . . not more, not less . . . the law of nourishment spontaneously results in development and growth. It expresses itself in a variety of ways. It is the spontaneous working of a natural law. You do not sit down with that law, and watch it, and worry about it. What you do is feed yourself, and leave all the rest to the law. If you violate the law, you will know it. But acting correctly in relation to it you will not fret and be stressed , you will simply take your meals and get on with your life. The result is that you are able to go on. You are able to work, play or do whatever. Why? Because you are nourished.

The Law of the Spirit of Life in Christ is like that. It is a law of life, and it works out in a very practical way when respected and adhered to. It works out spontaneously in certain directions. It has it own results that very naturally take place. The Law of the Spirit of Life in Christ is that spiritual law by which we become aware. That is the simplest way of putting it. The Lord Jesus knew that at certain times He could not act and could not speak. He had no movement of the Spirit in quickening. He had no life to do at that particular time. In His spirit there was no movement of life. The Law of the Spirit of Life was not active in the positive way. But when the Father, who knew what was required in speech or action saw that the time had come, He did not bend down and speak with an audible voice into His ear and say, *"Now is the time. Say this. Do that."* He simply quickened Him inwardly. The Law of Life became active in that direction, and He knew by an inward quickening what the mind of the Father was. That is what Paul meant when he says, **"The mind of the Spirit is life . . . "** (Romans 8:6).

If you want to know the mind of the Spirit about anything, you will know it by quickening. If you want to know what the Spirit is against, you will know it because there is death in your spirit in that direction. That means that you know the Lord, you know the Spirit, and you know what it means to move on the basis of the Law of the Spirit of Life in Christ Jesus. The Father governed Him by that

Law. He governs us by that exact same Law when we are joined to the Lord. Guidance is a matter of life **in the Spirit** and of life **by the Spirit**. The Lord Jesus had His life ordered, governed, conducted and arranged in every detail by the quickening Spirit.

This is what, again, provides the contrast. The Jews came along and said: *"Here is the Scripture . . . the Scripture says you should not do certain things, and you are doing them . . . you are wrong because the Scripture says this!"* **When Christ so acted was He violating the Scriptures? Or was He giving the Father's meaning to the Scripture?** When God gave that Law, did He not have a fuller meaning than what men see just on the surface? Was there not a spiritual interpretation? Was it not pointing forward to something, which when it came was to supercede – I do not mean break, but transcend – simply because higher, fuller and deeper meaning was reached? Christ is God's Sabbath. It is in Christ that the Father comes to rest in all His works. But they said, *"You must abide by the letter."* I purposely put it that way to show the difference between taking the letter and having the Holy Spirit's illumination of the letter. **"Life"** and **"the letter"** are often contrasted in the Word. *"The letter killeth, the Spirit maketh alive."*

I wonder if recognizing this fact, which should be very clear from what has been said, that this life which God gives by His Spirit, is not just a deposit in us. It is a gift, but not just a gift. If I were to take a dollar and give it to you, you would take it, say thank you and put it in your pocket. It will stay there with all the values that a dollar has. It will accomplish all that a dollar can accomplish, but it is in your pocket. You have it. It is a gift. You even said, thank you, when you got it. You realize there is a value bound up with that dollar as you carry it in your pocket. The day may come when, in an emergency, that dollar will get you out of a crisis. That crisis day may still be in your future. That may be likened to eternal life. The gift of God is eternal life through Jesus Christ our Lord. We say, *"Thank You Lord for eternal life."* It may be received and, as it were, put away, with the thought that one day it will save us from hell and get us to heaven. **Is that all that eternal life is meant to be?** No! Life is not just a gift, not just a deposit to be stored away. There is so much more to it than that. It has to do with all that I have been speaking about. The entire course of our life is governed by this Divine life. That life is God's basis of ruling, or ordering and of revelation. We shall only have a growing knowledge of the Lord through and by that life. Revelation to the believer is only on the basis of Divine life. The increase of that life means the increase of light, for light comes by life. ***"In Him was life, and the life was the light of men."***

Relationship Established by Resurrection Oneness

All that needs to be said at this point is that this relationship and fellowship with the Lord is available to all who are on resurrection ground or in resurrection union with the Lord. His risen life is for us today. If that is so, then all that that life means is for us also. Fellowship with the Father in life unto increase. Secret knowledge of the Lord. They are for us today!

I really desire you to see and understand that. One of the great needs today, at least in the case of those related to the Lord by the possession of eternal life through new birth, is the personal knowledge of the Lord . . . of having the inner life governed by the Lord . . . of having the inner intelligence of the Lord . . . His mind, His time and His way. It is very possible to simply be a Christian and live upon all that is external to oneself of Christianity. That, however, is quite another thing.

Do you know the Lord personally for yourself? Do you know what personal fellowship with the Lord is? Do you know what it is to have the Lord quicken you inwardly in relation to His mind about things, so that there is no need for anyone to tell you when something is wrong or not of the Lord. So that you don't need another to tell you what you ought to do in certain matters, or what is not becoming to a follower of Christ Jesus. It is God's will for you to so walk in fellowship and relationship with Him so that you will know . . . you will know from Him. He desires your life to be ordered and governed by that inner life and inner knowledge that that life gives.

I find it very remarkable to see how those who have their lives conformed to the mind of the Lord obey Him in the ordinary daily things of life. Things such as behavior, speech and actions. Life governs everything, and that life causes a ***"putting off"*** of things which are not according to Christ. There is an adjustment and they just drop away. There is no need to tell anyone in whom the Lord's life is active, in whom the Spirit of Life is governing, whether they ought to do certain things or to go to certain places. The Spirit of Life will govern and direct them by that inner life. How often I am asked about certain practices or places and reluctantly when my counsel was given the individual has said, *"Well, I knew before I asked. I just wanted to be sure."* How did they know? It was the Law of the Spirit of Life in Christ making them know. They know that if they perused a certain line or direction, that that was death, that was a check in their spirit, and that the witness of life lay in another direction. They also found that as they vacillated and wavered, as they postponed the deliberate obedience to the law of life that they began to enter into confusion and lost their peace and testimony.

This relationship and fellowship is common to all who are in risen union with Christ, to all who are partakers of His risen life . . .but it demands recognition. Do you recognize that it is for you individually? It demands recognition! You have to look this thing in the face and say, *"A life governed by the Spirit of God is mine. . .it is for me! It is not just for a few special people, it is for me!"* Life is the common basis of all believers. It is not just the basis for the privileged few or the more mature. ***"For in one Spirit were we all baptized into one body . . . "*** Do you recognize that fact? **Then it demands obedience!** We must be certain that we have no controversy with the Spirit of Life. We must be sure that there is no avoidance of, or resistance to, the Spirit of Life . . . and that equally we are not neglecting the dictates of the Spirit of Life, but are obedient in every part.

Not only must we shun a position of positive resistance, but we must give equal diligence not to slip into a careless one where our attitude becomes something like: *"Well, it is all right . It really doesn't matter very much."* **It does matter!** It is possible for death to begin to take hold and work without our even being aware of it happening. It works so subtly that we do not realize what has happened, until we wake up and find that we are a long way from the Lord, and have a tedious path to travel back, plus a lot to encounter along the way. It is a very costly thing to recover ground like that. The Law of the Spirit of Life in Christ demands active obedience and not just passive assent.

This demands a walk in the Spirit. That implies a **"going on,"** and that walk represents not only abiding in a certain realm, but also development or progress in what that realm represents. We need to understand that no one knows the mind or will of God perfectly. Please do not think that what I have been saying means that because we have Divine life we automatically know what the Lord wants in every detail. I doubt whether there is a person in this world who has that measure of knowledge. There will always be those things about which we will wait and pray as to the Lord's mind . . . things for which the time has not yet come for us to know it, or related to which some further factor remains in our knowing of the Lord that has to be dealt with first before such knowledge can be ours. We do not come to perfect knowledge of His times, and His directions, His thoughts and His deeds all at once . . . but we have the Law of Life, and as we move with the Lord we become more and more sensitive to that Law, and therefore more and more able to judge what the Lord's mind is. It is a progressive and growing thing. We must walk in the Spirit, and as we do we shall prove progressively and continuously **"what is that good, and perfect, and acceptable will of God."**

Do you see what is available to us? The nature of our relationship with the Lord . . . the tremendous power of life . . . the secret source which is ours through that life, and how through that life we are governed by the Lord. May He establish in us His Law of the Spirit of Life in Christ Jesus.

Chapter VII

The Hidden Manna

Scripture Lesson: John 4:31-34; 6:28-32, 34, 38,53-58; 7:17

(FD 290-20)

In verses 32 and 34 of the fourth chapter of the Gospel before us there are certain implicit facts. The **first** is that of a secret source of strength — *"I have meat to eat that ye know not . . . "* **Second**, there is shown to exist a link between the will of God and this secret strength. **Third**, we see that the strength of Christ is maintained in relation to the will of God. **Fourth,** there is shown to be a link with a Divine purpose, the complete fulfillment of which is alone true satisfaction, in much the say way that food is satisfaction to the body when in need. If the body craves food, and is utterly satisfied only by food suitable to its need, the same truth holds good here in relation to God. That is to say, there is a Divine purpose, and the complete accomplishment of that purpose is the only way of answering to the deepest need. It is the only way of bringing complete satisfaction, and of removing the pangs of hunger and transcending all the attendant weakness.

Obedience: the Way to Fulness

In all that has been said, one thing is perfectly clear: **obedience is the way of fullness.** By these Scriptures the food question is brought into view, and its elements are very simple. One is the maintaining of life. Another is satisfaction of need. Yet another is that of growth, of increase, of development, of progress and maturity. It is the attaining unto the full measure. Carrying those principles over into the realm of the spiritual, we can see how important the food question is to the inner man. You do not eat one meal for the rest of your life. Spiritually interpreted that means that the Lord does not want us to be just saved, but desires us to grow. Children of God who are under-nourished and undeveloped are a terrible tragedy.

In trying to determine why so many who accept Christ in the great evangelistic crusades fall away within the first three months, it was determined that this tragedy happens because there is no spiritual food to build them up. They have no ministry and no help beyond what can lead them to simple faith in the Lord Jesus. They were not directed to a local church where there was a strong Word ministry that could provide that necessary spiritual food. Hence, they fall away. If that is true, then it underscores yet more a further demand for the ministry of Christ in fulness.

Apart from those who backslide, what about those who, while not backsliding, never go on? May the cause not be the same? Surely there is no justification for condemning a ministry which is wholly given to feeding the flock, to the meeting of the need of that kind. The food question is a very acute and serious one. That is true in the natural, and it is also true in the spiritual . . . and perhaps with far more serious consequences.

The Nature of the Food That Others Know Nothing of

What do I mean by the food of God, the meat of God or the bread of God? — In answer to that question we must first think of and observe the Lord Jesus in His life here on planet earth. Then we shall see that what was true of Him here is also to be true of us. His basis of life is to be our basis. His resources of life are available to us.

Looking at Him in this light, note the following statements: *"I have meat to eat that ye know not . . . " "My meat is to do the will of Him that sent me, and to accomplish his work." "As the living Father hath sent me, and I live because of the Father . . . "* I only quote a portion of the last verse because the latter part has to do with us. *"I have meat . . . " "My meat is to do the will of him that sent me . . . " "I live by the Father . . . "* These words clearly mean that. His relationship with the Father was connected with a Divine purpose for the sake of which He was here on earth. His life in every detail was governed by a specific expression of the will of His Father. Simply put, it meant that the will of God for Him meant and represented a specific work. For that work He had come and to that work He had dedicated Himself. However, **in doing that work He needed to be sustained**. That sustenance was found in a maintained fellowship with the Father on all matters. As that fellowship with the Father on all practical matters was maintained He was able to go on . . . and on . . . and on! He was able to run without being weary and walk without fainting. There was being given to Him in a secret way supplies of strength, sustenance and nourishment. The will of the Father was comprehensive as to a purpose and detail . . . as to times, and methods and means.

(FD 290-21)
Not only was He one with the Father in the Father's objective and intention, but also in His method of reaching that objective, as well as in His times in the working out of that objective.

It is one thing to have a conception or apprehension of the purpose of God and to be totally dedicated to it, but it is quite another thing to know **HOW** God will realize or accomplish His purpose. It is still another thing to know the means He would employ. There are many who have a true conception of what God's purpose is . . . but the means they employ are not God's means. The way in which they do the work is not His way, and therefore they find that the Lord does not support them. They may be in a true direction, but being out of fellowship with the method or the means, they are compelled to take responsibility for the work themselves. They have to find their own resources. Result . . . they find themselves exhausted and brought to a standstill. They must resort to all kinds (of questionable) methods and means to raise the resources to carry on the Lord's work because they are not in the real enjoyment of His support. The work of God becomes a burden upon their shoulders and the Lord cannot order it otherwise because there is not the fullest fellowship between them and His ways, His methods, His means, His times and the details of His purpose.

In the case of the Lord Jesus it was quite the contrary. He was in secret fellowship with the Father concerning the details. With Him this represented a detailed obedience unto one comprehensive purpose. The only explanation needed by Him in any given matter was simply that of knowing that the Father willed it . . . and without further word He did it. That was the basis of His relationship. We never find in Him any sign of questioning why a thing should be done in a certain way, or at a certain time and not another, or why certain means should be employed and not others. It was enough that the Father willed it. The explanation came in the justification and vindication that followed. Doing the will of God was a matter of that obedience which never moves out from self and always out from the Father. As that was always true in His case, the spiritual resources of sustenance, maintenance, strength and energy were supplied.

The Secret of Growth and Rest

Abiding in the will of God was also the secret of His growth. Perhaps the growth of the Lord Jesus is something about which we have to be careful, and yet, while perfect in His moral nature and sinless as to His essential Being, the Word makes it perfectly clear that there was a progressiveness in His life. The Word states that He was made perfect through sufferings and that **"though He were a Son yet learned He obedience by the things which He suffered."** That is a difficult statement and I do not profess to understand all that it means, but it at least indicates that there was progressiveness in Him. There was progress from a **"perfect"** state to a **"perfected"** state. You cannot explain that, but we have the Word for it. He moved forward with the Father, but that forward movement was by development and expansion. It was the reaching of a point of fulness by one who has started at the beginning. He had laid aside the fullness or prerogatives of His Deity for His humanity or manhood. It was His by right, and was retained for Him, and as the Son of God He was still in possession of it, but as the Son of Man He relinquished the right to command the resource of Deity, and had accepted a life of complete dependence upon the Father. Because of that fact, His life was a life of faith . . . as is ours! His steps were steps of faith, which brought Him into an increase, and when He finished His course He was filled with all the fulness of a Divine replenishment of perfected humanity. We behold a Man filled with the fulness of God! In Jesus crowned we see not only God, but Man filled with the fulness of God, into which fulness we are also called. This is made very clear in the Epistles.

The truth of these statements is seen in such passages as ***Philippians 2:6-9: "Who being in the form of God, counted it not a thing to be grasped to be on equality with God, but emptied Himself, taking the form of a servant being made in the likeness of men; and...he humbled Himself becoming obedient even unto death, yea, the death of the cross. Wherefore also God highly exalted him (because of this obedience), and gave unto him the name which is above every name ..." (ASV)*** Then there follows the universal acknowledgment of Him in His exaltation: ***"That in the name of Jesus every knee should bow, of things in heaven, and things on earth, and things under the earth."*** Again in Hebrews 2 we read: ***"...we behold him who hath been made a little lower than the angels, even Jesus, because of the suffering of death*** (that is humiliation and emptying), ***crowned with glory and honor ..." (v 9)***. That is but another way of saying, **"filled with glory and honor"**. We can now see that in Christ there was a moving by obedience toward ultimate fulness. There was a progression. God was filling Him as He obeyed. That is what it means. Fulness was coming to Him as He obeyed. **The way of obedience is the way of fulness!**

The food, then, is the doing of the will of God. And to do the will of God is to abide in a relationship in which nothing is done without consultation with the Father. It not only means to inquire as to the Lord's will in some emergency, some turning point in life or in some crisis...but to have the entire life governed by God, so that everything is submitted to Him and brought under His Divine hand. In that life there is no loss or restriction, but rather development, growth, increase, enlargement, satisfaction and a coming into Divine fulness. There is no deeper satisfaction than that which is resultant from knowing that the Lord is satisfied and well pleased. To know that the Lord's will has been done, and not to have a shadow of doubt about it gives deep contentment to one's heart. No good meal ever satisfied the body of a man more than the knowledge that the Lord's will has been done.

This accounts for the remarkable tranquility in the life of the Lord Jesus. You can never find any anxiety, stress or strain in Him. He seemed to always be in a realm of spiritual content. That does not necessarily mean that He was always content with external things. See Him upsetting the tables of the money changers in the Temple, for example. However, deep down in His inner man there was a rest, and that rest was the result of His utter abandonment to the will of the Father, as well as His knowledge that the Father's will was being done hour by hour. There was no self-complacency in Him, rather the witness of the Spirit of Life as well as the witness of His Father: *"In Thee I am well pleased!"* So we are able to see that His life of obedience led Him progressively on unto fulness.

The Believers Participation

(FD 290-22)

That brings our relationship with Him into view, and explains most of the sixth chapter of John's Gospel. It foreshadows **union with Christ in resurrection life**. Union with Christ in resurrection life is set forth as spiritual feeding: *"He that eateth my flesh and drinketh my blood..." "Except ye eat the flesh of the Son of Man and drink His blood, ye have not life in yourselves ..."* What does that mean? — Verses 4 and 5 reveal the background to this chapter. *"Now the Passover, the feast of the Jews, was at hand ..."* At this time, the feeding question was very much in view. It was the time when they would feed upon the Pascal Lamb; for the Passover was a meal. So when feeding upon this special lamb was in view, we have the presence of a hungry multitude. You see the timing of God in everything. Here is a hungry multitude, and the thought of Passover feeding before them. At that very point, Jesus steps in and performed a miracle, feeding them as from a secret source. As to the feeding of the multitude the question had arisen: **"Whence bread enough for so great a multitude?"** The *"whence"* was a mystery. Bread was provided, but it did not come from a local bakery. In fact, in its fulness it did not even come from the little boy's lunch box. There was a hidden source in heaven. The multitude was fed, with bread to spare. A large surplus left over. There is much revelation truth here. Twelve baskets left over. Twelve disciples distributing the food to the hungry multitude. They that preach the Gospel shall live by the Gospel! The greater

truth is that there is more in God's secret storehouse than you and I need. When our immediate need is met, there is always a surplus. We need to be thankful that it is so!

Notice verse 27: *"Work not for the meat which perisheth, but for the meat which abideth unto eternal life, which the son of man shall give unto you."* In a short while the Lord will tell us what that means, but for the moment He says: *". . .for him the Father, even God, hath sealed."* This is said to a hungry multitude, with the Passover meal in view. The Lord Jesus steps in right at that point with His secret, heavenly source of sustenance, and then goes on to teach that He Himself is to be the source of supply for their deeper need — *"...for him the Father, even God, hath sealed."* He has taken them to the Passover. **What happens at the time of the Passover?** Every household takes a lamb without spot or blemish. Who is the judge of that? Who is to say that this lamb is or is not satisfactory? — The priest carries that responsibility. So it was in the case of all the sacrifices which were offered to God. The sacrifice was brought to the priest, who was an expert in discovering blemishes, and after his examination had been carried out, the sacrifice was declared to be in accordance with the standard required by God. When it was determined to be without spot, wrinkle, blemish or any such thing, the priest sealed it with the temple seal. **It was sealed as satisfactory according to God's mind.** Nothing could pass until the seal was on it. Nothing could be offered to God without that seal. Apply that in particular to the Passover lamb. It has to be sealed if it is to be God's sustenance. The slaying of it means that the lamb is acceptable to God on God's standard. With what fulness of meaning do the words fall on our ears: *"In Thee I am well pleased!"*

"...for him the Father, even God, hath sealed." Sealed by the Holy Spirit in the hour when God said: *"In thee am I well pleased."*

Permit me to go off on a tangent (for a moment) and go to the word of the Apostle: *"Whereby ye are sealed with the Holy Spirit of promise ..." (Ephesians 1:13).* What is the seal? — Accepted in the Beloved. Justified in Christ: perfect acceptance, because of what He is and of what we are in Him. God is well pleased. God is satisfied.

I am back! Here is Christ, sealed to be God's Own satisfaction, and therefore given as God's satisfaction to His people. He has done the will of God perfectly when He becomes the Passover Lamb. Because the will of God has been perfectly done and God has been perfectly satisfied, He gives Christ, Who is His satisfaction, for our satisfaction. That is union with Christ and our eating of Him. It is faith taking Christ in resurrection life to become our energy. He becomes our energy, our vitality, our strength and our sustenance when our relationship to Him is exactly the same as that which existed between Him, as Man, and the Father. *"As the living Father sent me, and I live because of the Father; so he that eateth me, he shall live also because of me" (John 6:57 ASV).* How did He live by the Father? — By taking the Father's mind, the Father's will, the Father's thoughts, desires and intentions to be the basis of His entire life. On that ground the Father gave Himself to Him in life. Now, having perfectly satisfied the Father, and having become the Father's full satisfaction, He becomes the basis of our life. We live by Him! Christ our life! Christ our sustenance! What does that mean? — It simply means that in Christ are found all those vital moral and spiritual elements which we require to live upon. They are provided for us. This perfection of Christ is a living energy, a vital force. It is something that comes to us in the power of the Holy Spirit in a living way.

Man According to the Divine Mind

(FD 290-23)

Notice that in John 6:53 the reference is to Christ as Man – *"Except ye eat the flesh of the <u>Son of man</u> and drink his blood, ye have not life in yourselves."* What is the meaning of that designation? — It speaks of man perfected according to God's mind. There is only one such man, the Man Christ Jesus, and it is because of what He is as Man according to God's mind (and through our faith union with Him, and faith's drawing upon Him) that moral and spiritual strength is imparted to us. It is very difficult to define or explain the mystery of how Christ gives Himself to us through faith . . .but it is a fact. The difference is between our effort, struggle and wrestling to overcome, and our taking His overcoming by faith, to meet every situation, both within and without, on the basis of what Christ has already done and of what He now is. This, my friend, is the foundation that God has put beneath our feet in Christ risen.

God has put full and final accomplishment of everything under our feet. To change the metaphor, He has spread a table with every commodity that we need for our spiritual life, and we may draw upon that bounty as we will. Christ is provided as the bread from heaven, the perfection of moral victory, of spiritual ascendency, and our part is to learn how to live on the basis of what Christ is. *"I live because of the Father ..." "He that eateth me, he also shall live because of me..."* The alternatives which are presented are whether we will try to proceed in our relation to the will of God on the basis of what we are by nature, governed by our natural resources and the conditions that may exist in spirit, soul and body at any time. . .or whether we are going to recognize that there is another secret source which is more than that, and which is the source of certain victory and triumph, and live on that. *"He that abideth in me, and I in him, the same beareth much fruit: for apart from me ye can do nothing."* In those words spoken in the parable of the Vine and the branches, the Lord sets forth this truth about which I am speaking.

What is abiding? — Abiding in Christ is the opposite of abiding in ourselves. To abide in ourselves is simply to try to live and work for the Lord in and by ourselves. It is the asking of the Lord to help "us" to do it, instead of recognizing that a life wholly pleasing to God has been lived and that faith appropriates that accomplishment in Christ. Abiding in Christ is simply doing everything as out from Christ. This is the only sure ground. There is no need to even ask, *"Can it be done? Can I do it?"* In Christ it is done! The Lord Jesus has met everything that you or I will meet, and in all things has already done what is needful. That is available to faith, and faith says: *"In myself this thing is absurd, and to attempt it would be ridiculous. It is even silly to contemplate it. But it can be done, because it has already been done. I can meet this demand, and I can stand up to that other one. I can go through this. I can do that because,* **I can do all things through Christ which strengtheneth me.** *"* It is what Christ is as our secret source of strength, of sustenance and of nourishment.

We are in the School of the Spirit and we learn this lesson in a progressive way. He learned, and we learn, though in our case there is a difference to be noted. We are learning to draw upon the fulness which He consummated. We are working out from a fulness as we press forward toward the goal. We are learning how to come back to a fulness whereas He moved toward a fulness. For Him, the Cross was the end. . .for us, it is the beginning. It is imperative that we learn how to come back to His fulness, and we learn progressively, step by step like little children. First of all, learning to walk and to talk. Like children, we are confronted with things which we have never done or even attempted before. We are confronted with things that are new and strange to us. For a child, the contemplation of taking a first step is a very terrifying proposition. We are brought into this realm of faith where at the beginning, like a baby taking that first step, sometimes scares us almost to death. But there are arms stretched out, and those arms represent for us the accomplishment of what is required of us. . .the thing is done.

The strength is available for the task at hand. It is a strength which has been proven over and over again. Recognizing those outstretched arms, we learn to walk by Christ. . .and the next time we will be able to go further. Each time capacity is being enlarged, and we are coming to a fuller measure of maturity. Eventually the fulness of Christ will be that all that Christ accomplished will be made good in us. *"All." "I can do all things ..."* Whether at home or abroad, it will be done!

I do not know that we have ever yet caught a glimpse of what a perfect humanity is going to be like. A perfect humanity in glory hereafter will be one of tremendous capacity and tremendous ability. The accomplishments and achievements of that perfect humanity will be the occasion of great wonder. **CHRIST IN FULNESS!**

The Offense of the Cross

Remember that this way is a way that is a constant offense to the flesh, to the natural man. The Jews argued with one another, saying, *"How can this man give us his flesh to eat?"* But not only did the Jews, the religious people in their religious satisfaction, strive together, but it is also written, *"Many therefore of his disciples, when they heard this, said, This is a hard saying; who can hear it?"* At times, even disciples could not go on. When they came face to face with the implications of such a saying, they were no longer willing to be associated with Him on a basis of that kind. The flesh loves to be in charge. It loves to make the plans, arrange the program, organize the work and get it done. It revels in that. However, when you come and say to the whole order of things, **THE WAY OF GOD IS THE WAY OF UTTER DEPENDENCE AND FAITH, WITH THE HOLY SPIRIT IN CHARGE**, and you must keep your hands off and be willing to do only what the Lord tells you and no more (that is the meaning of *"I can do nothing out from myself"*), it is an offense to the natural man! It would seem that we meet with that daily, do we not?

That is the difference between meeting together as they did at Antioch to pray things through and get the Lord's witness as to His will, and having a committee meeting to discuss a proposal and make plans. If the natural man is not running the show, if he is not arranging everything, ordering everything and doing everything, he feels that no progress can possibly be made. The naturally minded Christian thinks that unless you come forth with **"your"** plans, and announce **"your"** program, and declare what **"you"** are doing . . .then nothing is being done.

The whole accomplishment of God in Christ is on the basis of Divine life mediated through faith. That is simply another way of saying, **"Christ has to be the basis of everything in a spiritual way."** This is an offense to the flesh, but a satisfaction to the Spirit.

Final Word

This chapter is called **"The Hidden Manna"**. That is a word spoken to the Church at Pergamum in Revelation 2:17 - *"To him that overcometh. . .will I give of the hidden manna ..."* Why was that said? — Because the people of that church were indulging in feeding upon the sacrifices of paganism. Do you perceive the character of the idol sacrifices of paganism? They had the counterfeit principle. These mystic rites of paganism in the eating of sacrifices offered to gods meant that there was an imbibing of the powers of the gods. There we have a true principle carried into a demonic realm, associated with all the evil things. . .and Christians were eating of sacrifices offered to idols, to demons, to nourish their spiritual life in a mystic way. Think of it! They have grasped the idea — we get strength from the gods! **It was spiritual strength they were after, but they went into the wrong realm to get it!**

To the one who needs spiritual strength, the Lord says: *"...to him that overcometh, to him will I give of the hidden manna ..."* The hidden manna is Christ is heaven! The thought carries us back to the Most Holy Place in the tabernacle where the Ark of the Covenant abode. In the Ark was a pot of manna. . .hidden in the Ark of the Most Holy Place. Did you get that. . .**HIDDEN IN THE MOST HOLY PLACE!** Earlier when speaking about the opened heaven we saw that the Most Holy Place represented heaven. The Holy Place represented earth. The manna in the Most Holy Place typifies Christ in heaven. *"I am the bread of life. . .I am come down from heaven ..."* Seven times in the discourse in John 6 the phrase *"down from heaven"* is used. Christ in heaven is the Hidden Manna, the secret source of sustenance.

I am struggling to explain the inexplicable and to define the indefinable. One can never adequately explain the mystery of how Christ becomes the spiritual strength and nourishment of His own, but the fact is there. The practical course left to us is to act upon the fact that Christ is our sufficiency, no matter what the demand. . .and never to fall back upon what we are in ourselves or make our natural condition or circumstances the ground of decision. That is not the criterion, that is not the conclusion of the matter. *"Not what I am, O Lord, but what Thou art,"* must rule in the presence of need. In the obedience of faith, we must step out on Him. We are brought to the conclusion of John 6: **that the work of God and the will of God is to believe in Him whom He hath sent.**

What does it mean to believe in Him? How do we believe in Christ when we feel bad, when we feel ill or when things are difficult? — the answer has been given. This belief, as we see borne out by this story is appropriation. It is eating. It is one thing to say you believe in certain foods, but here that passive kind of belief has no place. Belief in this food involves the taking or partaking of it. May the Lord show us the meaning of the secret source of strength.

CHAPTER VIII

Peace: The Cessation of Againstness

Scripture Lesson: Matthew 11:28-30; John 8:32, 36; 14:27; 16:33 20:19, 21, 26

(FD 290-24)

It does not require a very profound study of the earthly life of our Lord Jesus to discover that it was characterized by a wonderful peace of spirit and restfulness of heart all the way through. There are some things strikingly absent from His life. Dr. S. D. Gordon has said that *"Jesus was never known to have run, or it is not recorded that He ever ran."* The point being that He was never in a state of emergency or that He was never hurried. He was never found in a state of anxiety or fretfulness. In short, there was nothing in Him that was the opposite of perfect tranquility. This does not suggest that there was not a great deal to make for a state of anxiety or fretfulness. There was much to make it other than it was. **He was in many storms. . .but the storm was never in Him!** There were continuous demands made on Him. Day and night. There was much labor to be done. It would seem that one day in His life held within it enough to be spread over a far longer period in the ordinary person's life, yet He was never perturbed or distressed. He never lost His calm or His cool. He was Master of every situation.

It was when the things which make for unrest were nearest Him, that He spoke about peace and rest. It was as He was moving into the final scenes of His life, knowing all that He was about to go through in His Cross and knowing all that the Cross with its suffering and death would mean, that He said to His disciples: **"Let not** *your heart be troubled ..."* and again a second time: ***"Let not your heart be troubled, neither let it be afraid ..."***

All that lies on the surface and does not need proving. But we need to attempt to understand the nature of His peace, His rest and His wonderful liberty. It seems that there were several matters in which He had rest which made Him different from all other men. As this study has been showing, it was the secret sources of His life which constituted the difference between Him and all others. He was unique among men, but there was a reason for it. The reason was the background of His life. . .a background in which there were secret resources. It would seem that the matter of peace, rest, tranquility and ascendency were closely connected with two or three of the major issues of life.

Peace in the Face of Temptation

The first of these issues is SIN. We know very well that it is through sin that peace is lost and rest is destroyed. It is because of sin that fret, worry, care and anxiety find a dwelling place in our lives. There was no sin in Him, but that fact does not carry us totally to the solution. It would be easy for us to say, *"Well, there being no sin in Him, He knew nothing whatever of the stresses, strains and struggles with which we have to deal because of sin in us. He knew nothing of all that realm of conflict, battle and worry which we know because of what is in our natures."* If that were the truth, He would be so far removed from our fears and struggles and would not be able to have any practical, experimental sympathy with us. Instead we are told that He is able to succor the tempted, on the ground that He Himself has been tempted in all points like as we, yet apart from sin.

The other half of the truth about Him is that He was pressed to take actions which, because of their relatedness, would have been wrong. There was no sin in Him, but strong pressure was brought to bear in an effort to cause Him to do things which were wrong. For example, He was capable of suffering. Because of that fact, He was bound to be pressured to spare Himself, but to have done so, because of all that which was related, would have been wrong. Anyone who is capable of suffering is at least capable of having a suggestion made to him that he can find a way of avoiding it. Because of the reality of the suffering, the suggestion has point. It is not pointless, it finds a point of contact. It makes an appeal. **We must remember that temptation is not sin.** An **appeal** to take a course which would be wrong is not sin. Not until we have consented to the temptation have we sinned. I know that is very elementary, but it is necessary to understanding the situation.

It was not only in the matter of suffering that He registered temptation, but in many other ways also. Temptation was presented to Him. He was tempted. Temptation is not temptation if it comes up against something which has no capacity of knowing its meaning. If you talk to me in a language that I do not understand, I register nothing. It means nothing to me at all. There is nothing in me that can in any way respond to it. In referring to His being tempted of the devil, if we said that it was impossible for Him to yield to or consent to it, we would be talking nonsense. He was capable of suffering and therefore He was capable of being tempted to take a course of direction which would have saved Him from suffering . . .and that was temptation. The temptation that came to Him was not pointless, but rather temptation which had to be positively resisted with a strength of will. The enemy would not assail me with temptations if they could not come near me. The Lord Jesus had to take a definite, deliberate attitude of resistance.

Since the temptation was real, how was it that He was able to continue on in peace and rest without succumbing? Without being stressed? Without losing that peace and rest? — The simple answer is that **He was totally abandoned to the Father's will**, so that the temptation itself was defeated by or through His complete loyalty. Those things are evidenced as we read of His specific temptations. His defense was His loyalty to His Father. His abandonment to the Father's will saved Him from any of those disturbances which come by letting in questions of doubt, or by responding in any way to a subtle suggestion of Satan.

The secret of His peace was His oneness with His Father. It was this that made Him different from all others. It was separateness from God which meant that they could not meet and deal with sin, either within or without, and go on their way triumphantly. His union with the Father meant that while He was tempted in all points like as we are, with Him there never came about a situation of sin which robbed Him of His peace, which destroyed His rest and which brought Him into bondage.

Peace in His Being and Nature

(FD 290-25)

We now come to **the second aspect of His peace**. It is intimately connected with His own being and nature. The personality of Christ was a united one; His was a united soul, that is, His mind was not two, but one. There were no double reasonings with Him. There was no conflict between His own reason and the Father's reason. His was a united mind. . .it was **"one mind"** (let this mind be in you which was also in Him). His heart was single. There were no divided desires. There was no conflict with the Father's desires. His will was one. One will with the Father's will, not in identity, but in fellowship. He will speak of **"My will"**, and **"Thy will"** as two separate things. ***"Father, not My will, but Thy will be done ..." "I came not to do mine own will, but the will of Him that sent Me ..."***. Here are two wills, and yet those two wills are so blended together that in effect, purpose, objective and sympathy they become one. This oneness resulted in the uniting of His very being.

Let us once again note the nature of His temptations which came to Him. All the temptations which came to Him, and there were many more than the three listed in the wilderness, were intended to create a division between Him and His Father. You can see that in every instance. They were intended to cause Him to move out of oneness with the Father and act or speak on His own. They were attempts to induce Him to act independently of His Father. Satan desired to bring about a division in this unity or oneness. He knew that if he could make two where there was one he would have achieved with the Son of Man what he achieved with the first Adam. It was the oneness of His being, by virtue of the total union with the Father, and the ground of His undisturbed peace, which was the objective of the enemy's attack.

In the Greek the word **"peace"** simply means **"unity"** or **"concord"**. It does not mean a state or condition of quiet. That may be a result or an effect of peace, but it is not the meaning of the word. Peace is harmony, concord and unity. When He spoke of *"My peace"*, He was not merely offering a tranquil atmosphere, He was offering them a union with the Father, which would mean that the conflict, unrest and discord would cease. **Peace is the tranquility of oneness.** *"That they may be one, even as we are one ..." (John 17:22)* — oneness as in the Father and the Son. For Him, rest was the result of a united being. . .no strain or controversy with the Father. . .rather in total harmony and agreement with Him.

You may be saying, *"Yes, in His case that was very true. But it was so much easier for Him, seeing Who and what He was!"* But I must come back and again point out that there was another ground which is the common ground of all. . .His and ours. **What was the ground of this oneness, this harmony, this accord?** Was it merely His nature? Was it simply because He was God the Son, the Second Person of the Godhead? — No! There was an active cause or principle. What was it? This tranquility, this rest, this peace resultant from harmony, unitedness, oneness in His being was also resultant from **FAITH IN THE FATHER, AND FAITH IN THE FATHER'S FAITHFULNESS!** His anchor was the faithfulness of His Father.

That is common ground, not His alone. He may have had it in greater measure. He may have gone far ahead of us, but the principle of His life, is the principle our lives. He wrought this thing out for us, then went ahead of us traversing the same way in which we are to follow. So as His life was a life of faith in the Father and in the Father's faithfulness, so must ours be.

The fact that He suffered may raise a question. You may say, *"If anyone suffers or is capable of suffering, and the suffering is genuine. . .can suffering and peace go together?"* Yes, they can! He suffered so much that His countenance, His face, was marred more than any man's. You look upon that marred visage, that suffering, that scarred face, and you can see peace. Can that really be true? Is it possible that while going through agonies there can be peace? — It depends! He suffered according to the will of God, and that makes all the difference. There is suffering according to the will of God which means perfect peace and rest. Put that another way. . .perfect peace and perfect rest does not mean that we are going to be immune from suffering. Suffering marked Him, but it never distracted Him so that He lost His peace. . .I am referring to the suffering of His life. There was a moment when He lost a sense of the Father's face, one moment! For one small moment He was forsaken. In that moment His soul was rent, and there was despair. But for the rest of His life, in which the meaning of that moment was not so implicit, His life, while He suffered, was never distracted.

So the second thing is that His peace was because of a united heart, mind and will. Because of the oneness of His being and nature.

Peace in Relation to Lawful Obligation

(FD 290-26)

The third aspect is in relation to a legal obligation. What a realm of disturbed rest and peace that is! It was concerning that realm the He spoke those wonderful words in Matthew 11. *"Come unto me all ye that labour and are heavy laden, and I will give you rest. Take my yoke upon you, and learn of me; for I am meek and lowly in heart: and ye shall find rest unto your souls."* What was the yoke with which His was contrasted? It is inferred in the passage: *"They bind heavy burdens and grievous to be borne, and lay them on men's shoulders ..." (Matthew 23:4).* It was the heavy load of the Law, of legal obligation: *"Thou shalt!"* and *"Thou shalt not!"* and that split into a thousand fragments. There is no peace in that. There is no rest there. It was one ceaseless, endless concern lest the Law be broken at some point, and if it be broken in one point, responsibility for the whole was imposed. Once the Law was violated in one point, responsibility for the breaking of the entire Law was incurred. Legal obligation, as they knew it then, and as the Judaizers always imposed it upon men, became a grievous burden and a cause of lost rest. They had no rest. Some of them may have deceived themselves (as some do today!) into believing that they had rest. They may even have been living in a false realm like Saul of Tarsus, but in Romans 7 he eventually unveils his condition.

Again let us look at the Lord Jesus. Go through His life with the legal burden in view, and you will never see it resting on Him. The Jews believed that they were governed by the Law, and so far as they understood the Law, they were. If you took the mere letter of the Law, they were right, and according to them the Lord Jesus was the biggest Sabbath-breaker that they had ever met. How often did He do things on the Sabbath which caused all the trouble. Why would He persist in doing these things on the Sabbath? He knew what the effect of such actions would be. He had done this before, and there had been a terrific uproar. Yet He does another thing on the Sabbath. His disciples are walking with Him through the field on the Sabbath. . .and **He does not say**, *"Don't pick any corn and eat it today. You know what trouble it will cause with the Jews. And it is also forbidden by the Law."* They did it! And again, there was trouble. But He goes on in tranquility and rest. He is not in the least disturbed. Seemingly, He is breaking the Law. But in actuality He is immune from its burden of legal obligation. He is free and at rest and has no guilty conscience. Blessed state to be in!

If only we could be this way before God. If only we could be open, honest and transparent in truth. If only we could live with perfect, uninterrupted and unbroken communion with our Father. If only we could live our lives without a ripple of unrest upon the surface of our hearts, while we maintained the closest relationship with our God. How do you explain it? Is He wrong? Did He break the Sabbath according to the Law? — Well, according to the letter of the Law He did. But what was the nature of His breaking of the Law?

The Character and Objective of the Law

That brings us to the heart of things. For what was the Law given? Was it given arbitrarily? Was it given because God wanted to impose many restrictions upon men to satisfy some whim of His? I don't believe so! God is not frivolous! — the answer is that the Law was given in order to secure the rights and place of God. God had primary rights and primary place, and everything had to acknowledge, recognize and work in relation to that. God's rights and God's place could be set aside, and in the universe there existed a great rebellious intelligence that was set against God's rights and God's place. That great intelligence and power had secured a hold in man by man's consent and disobedience. The result was that man in his heart, in his nature and in his being, was joined with this great intelligence. God had to move to frustrate the success of man and Satan in their relationship, as their purpose was to evict Him out of His place and rob Him of His rights.

There were various ways in which the enemy could do that through man. The main way, which would include many things, would be **IDOLATRY**. Take the decalogue out of which all the other arises: *"Thou shalt have none other gods before me"*, and then follows, *"Thou shalt love the Lord thy God with all thy heart, and with all thy soul, and with all thy mind (thy strength)"*. That is the foundation of the Law. *"Thou shalt not make unto thee a graven image, nor the likeness of any form that is in heaven above, or that is in the earth beneath, or that is in the water under the earth: thou shalt not bow down thyself unto them, nor serve them ..."* That is the open, naked form of idolatry, which gives the devil an entrance to supplant God, and to rob Him of His rights of worship and of being the Supreme Object of worship. Follow the decalogue, and you find other forms of idolatry. *"Thou shalt not covet"* this, that, and the other. *"Covetousness which is idolatry" (Colossians 3:5).* How is it idolatry? — It is putting something in the place of the Lord. It is wanting something for itself. . .for your own possession. It is putting the Lord aside.

There are various other forms of idolatry, and there are other ways in which the Lord can be set aside and His rights taken from Him. The decalogue touched on them. Lust! What is lust? — It is that excessive desire which is for the gratification of self, and if self in the fallen man is not opposed to God what is? It may be lust for recognition, lust for reputation, lust for personal enlargement, lust for success, lust for influence, lust for power, or a thousand other things, but it is **self.** Self-satisfaction, self-glory, self-realization, self-fulness. . .these things give rise to all the other unholy things like jealousy and pride.

It you study it closely, you will see that all of this is simply God having His rights taken away, and His place usurped. The enemy gets in when self asserts its own will and way. He gets in along all lines of idolatry, and when he gets in, God's place is taken over. God will not occupy any heart or life with the Devil.

All the *"Thou shalt!"* and *"Thou shalt not!"* had a hidden meaning. It was not simply: Thou shalt not because thou shalt not! It was because of their ignorance of or the setting aside of the secret meaning, the something hidden in the command, that an opportunity was given to the adversary of God, as far as God's rights and God's place were concerned.

When Christ comes He establishes all those meanings in His own Person. The explanation of His life can be seen in this two-fold thing, that He establishes and secures the position of God, and all the rights of God. Here is a Man in Whom God's place is established beyond dispute. Fully and finally God has His place, and all God's rights are secured in Him. That is the meaning of His fight, that is the meaning of His stand in the temptations. It was for God's rights. **"It is written!" "It is written!" "It is written!"** And these things written represent spiritual truths, spiritual laws by which God's place and God's rights are secured. If the opposite of these things exist then God is robbed and put out, and man takes what belongs to God. Christ was having none of that in His Person. God was going to have everything so far as He was concerned. When Christ comes into the life, He secures God's place and God's rights completely.

Therefore, all mere forms of spiritual truths can be put away. The decalogue, or the Law, goes into obscurity just as the entire Old Testament typical system. All of the types of the Old Testament were only the Law in object lessons. They were the Law put into material form. The oral Law was: *"Thou shalt"*, and *"Thou shalt not"*. That was all summed up and expressed in a system of types. The Tabernacle was but an outward expression of spiritual principles, just as the Law was. When the Lord Jesus takes the place of the Tabernacle, the priest, the sacrifice, the altar. . .and everything else, and in Himself fulfills and establishes all that which was signified by the type, He also takes up the Law and fulfills all of its spiritual principles. When He has done that, the Tabernacle is finished . . .all of the types are finished. . .and the external Law is finished.

However, there now remains a spiritual reality!

Did the Lord Jesus, by anything which He did on the Sabbath day, ever displace or rob God of His rights? — To the contrary, it worked the other way. God was continually getting, not losing. The Lord Jesus was liberated from the lower by the higher. . .and so shall we be liberated from the lower by a higher law. Do you believe that anyone in whom Christ reigns supreme will ever do anything that would rob God, and put Him out of His rights and His place? You will not need an oral Law or a written Law if the Law of the Spirit of Life in Christ Jesus is dominant in you. That is why He said: *"Moses said. . .but I say..."* And when He put the *"but"* there He lifted things on to a much higher level. Moses said, If you do this thing you shall die! But I say unto you that, there is something more, there is a thinking. . .and if you think, you have virtually done. . .and you are just as responsible. It is a question of the heart . . . not of outward performance. Things have to go higher, and when you have the Spirit you are not in bondage to the mere outward form.

Resurrection Oneness with Christ

Do you see how all of this brings us to Resurrection-union with Christ? I have been stressing that resurrection-union with Christ is the dominant, active risen life of Christ in us. **What is the risen life of Christ?** — It is what He is in living power, energizing us. That will always be in a positive way. It will never be in the negative . . . thou shalt not.

Legalism can be very barren, very unfruitful, very hard, very cold and very unprofitable. Those who are still bound by the Law (either Jewish or Christian) are very often robbing God of much that He might otherwise have. The question is not, **"What sayeth the Law of Moses?"** What sayeth the Law? The Lord is greater than the Law, in the sense that He gets in the real depth of the Law as to its real spiritual meaning and value. And the meaning of the Law is that God comes into His rights and is given His place.

The letter to the Hebrews has much to say about rest: *"There remaineth therefore a rest for the people of God." "As I sware in my wrath, they shall not enter into my rest" (Hebrews 4:3, 9).* What is the context of all of that? What is the meaning and message of the letter to the Hebrews? Is it not that Christ has come, and all the types are gone? He fulfills all the types. Hebrews deals with the Tabernacle, the priests and the sacrifices in the light that Christ has come and now these types of Him are gone. Reality has finally come.

What was the type of this rest? — I think the land was the type of the rest, but Christ takes the place of the land. Just as He fulfills every other type so He fulfills that. The promise of the Father works out to the fulness of Christ. . .and it is a land full, flowing with milk and honey. It has every kind of resource that must be appropriated. Christ is that! He is the rest of God!

All of this is available to us in risen life-union with Christ. Is it a matter of the sin question disturbing rest? Christ has dealt with the sin question. We have remission of sins in His blood. We have deliverance by His Cross. Sin's penalty, guilt and power are met in Him. He has made Himself responsible for the sin question. Initially, He has borne all the sins of the past, and all the sins of the future. We stand in the good of that when we confess our sins. *"If we walk in the light as he is in the light we have fellowship...and the blood of Jesus Christ His Son cleanseth us (goes on cleansing us) ..."* Walking in the light! *"If we confess our sins he is faithful and just to forgive us our sins and to cleanse from all unrighteousness..."* He has made Himself responsible for all future sins as well as past, while we abide in Him and walk in the light. *"Our fellowship is with the Father, and with His Son ..."* There is no fellowship if the sin matter is not dealt with. *"Made peace through the blood of His Cross ..."* Through His life we come into the benefit of Christ's victory in the realm of sin.

Is it the matter of the oneness of personality, of life? The Spirit is the Spirit of His oneness. The Holy Spirit's work in us is to bring us into a oneness of being, oneness of heart, oneness of mind, and oneness of will with God...to get rid of the schism in us. The Spirit will woo, He will urge, but He will not strive. The flesh will be there, and it will war against the Spirit. In Galatians 5:17 where the reference is made to the fact there is a grievous mis-translation. The translation says: *"The flesh lusteth against the Spirit, and the Spirit against the flesh."* One word mis-translated there robs us of tremendous value. The original is: *"The flesh lusteth against the Spirit, but the Spirit lusteth against the flesh."* That *"but"* saves the whole situation. Yes, the flesh lusteth against the Spirit, but the Spirit lusteth against the flesh. Do you see the value of that? That is all to bring about in us this oneness, this unity, this accord, this harmony with God. **What is the work of the Spirit?** Basically, to put His finger upon things which are not in harmony with God's will, and to check us inwardly when and where we are out of accord. To be filled with the Spirit is to be wholly one with God.

Final Word

Is it in the matter of legal obligation? Well, we are emancipated, we are set free, by the Son, by being brought on to a higher level than that of the Law. Delivered by a higher Law. Saved unto rest, peace and liberty because God has His place and His rights in Christ. . .and Christ is in us. There will never be any working to take God out of His place, or to take His rights from Him, where Christ is Lord. Therefore there will be no need for, **"Thou Shalt!"** and **"Thou shalt not!"** The place where Christ is Lord is the place of liberty. Someone has said, *"When Christ is Lord, you can go where you like and do what you like."* Well. . .the one thing I want to say first is that **in Christ we have a new set of likes.**

The question is not, *"Shall I go here or there?* It is not, *"Shall I do it on this particular day or does the Law say, No?"* **The question is**, *"Will the Lord get something through this thing? Is the Lord going to get His place in this?* That is the principle upon which Christ acted. A man made whole on the Sabbath day! Was that to the glory of God? Certainly! Give God His place and there is life. That is the principle! Is the Lord going to gain or lose through this? We must get the witness from Him in our own hearts as to the issue of any situation. But if we are simply bound by legal observance we have missed the real Law of the Spirit of life. May He show us the meaning of life as the governing law, power and energy of our being. The risen life of the Lord as the perfect law of liberty.

CHAPTER IX

Understanding Sonship

Scripture Lesson: Matthew 11:27 and Luke 10:22

(FD 290-27)

I will be referring to other passages as we go along, but I would like to first draw your attention again to the fact that so many of the things about which I am speaking in connection with the meaning of the Lord's life come within the category of things which are definitely stated to be secrets. You have probably noticed that as we have continued. That is why I speak of those things as the **"secret resources"**. They are so often declared to be things which are not open to all. They are hidden. They seem to lie beneath, and cannot be apprehended on natural grounds. We now approach another matter which is definitely in that realm. It tells something of which no ordinary man has understanding. *"No one knoweth the Son, save the Father; neither doth any know the Father, save the Son, and he to whomsoever the son willeth to reveal him."* With that reminder let us turn to **John's Gospel. 1:18, 34; 3:34-36; 5:20, 22; 9:35-36; 11:4; 17:1 and Colossians 2:2.** Many more passages could be added, but these are sufficient to provide a basis upon which to proceed.

As in the case of each of the other matters which have been mentioned, we must turn to observe what this relationship meant to the Lord Jesus, and how it became a background of everything to Him. It gave meaning and value to all His utterances, all His acts and all His experiences. . .both for the present and for the future. How often He spoke of Himself in terms of Sonship, and of the

Father in personal relationship with Himself. This forms a strong and full basis for His life, and He continually drew upon it. In fact, we might say that it meant everything to Him throughout His entire earthly life.

Before we go further in meditating upon that, I must say a word about the two titles which He bore in Sonship. We are familiar with both of them — Son of Man! Son of God! The point at which these two titles or designations deviate has only to do with His work . . .not with His Person. It is very important to recognize that. We may not, we cannot divide the Person. That is what Paul means by ***"the mystery of God, even Christ"***, and we may dwell for an entire lifetime upon that mystery without being able to solve it. The Person of the Lord Jesus Christ has been the battleground from the beginning, and probably always be so long as time shall last. More heresies and errors have sprung from man's attempts at solving that mystery and presenting it for human apprehension than from any other source. It is always extremely delicate, if not dangerous, to attempt to handle the Person of Christ.

So the titles do not in any way make two Persons. Instead they represent two realms and two aspects of work, and therefore of truth. . .relative to the Person. We know what those realms are. As Son of Man He is Representative of man by vital union with man. As Son of God He is expressive of God by oneness with the very Person of God. That is technical and largely theological. It represents the two sides of the Person in practical expression and for practical purposes, as to His office and His work.

The Son of Man

(FD 290-28)

We must safeguard the title ***"Son of Man"***, so that we do not mentally, or perhaps unconsciously, bring it to a lower level and into a lesser realm than it should occupy. For even the title, ***"Son of Man"***, goes far beyond the thought of human birth. Along with the revelation that He was born of a virgin, we have this statement: ***"The Son of man which is in heaven ..." (John 3:13).*** That carries the designation higher than earth, and gives it a Divine meaning and a Divine value. Unless we recognize that we get into much confusion over the virgin birth of the Lord Jesus. For example, men have said that the theory of the virgin birth breaks down because it would relate all sin to man, and rule the whole question of sin out of woman. Can you not see how foolish such talk is? We must recognize that Christ was not born of a virgin on any natural basis . . .under any foolish conceit as that woman is sinless and man sinful, and thereby a virgin birth would secure His sinlessness. There was an intervening between all that Mary inherited and what Christ was by a sovereign act of the Holy Spirit.

Many such theological, doctrinal, and technical questions arise over the Person of Christ. My point is that even the title, **"Son of Man"**, makes Him different from the rest of men in a Divine sense, and that while **"Son of Man"**, is vitally related to man, He is different from the rest of men.

The Son of God

Then a word about the other title. There is a phrase that is unique to John's Gospel, namely, **"only begotten Son"**. Unless you know and remember one thing, that title is likely to cause some confusion. As you read through the New Testament, you find that others are begotten of God. John himself in his letters speaks about the sons begotten of God. How then is Christ the **"only begotten Son"**? You must remember that these words were written long after most of the New Testament had been written and circulated. By the time they were written there were multitudes of sons begotten of God, and yet the Apostle deliberately, and with precision wrote of **"the only begotten Son"**. This is not just a question of time, that Christ was the first, and being the first for a time was the only begotten Son. That would lower Him to the level of all the others, and in the process rule out a certain distinctiveness. So the explanation must lie elsewhere, for this word does not mean that Christ was the only one who was begotten of God. It does not especially relate to the begetting at all, but rather to **the kind of begotten**.

It could be accurately translated, **"the uniquely or singularly begotten"**. It means that there was never another one like this One. He is the only such One, this begotten of God. The emphasis is not upon the **"begetting"**, but upon the *"only"* — *"**the only begotten . . .the uniquely begotten**"*. It is a very interesting word. If you take the time to study it, you discover that it is often seen to occupy a place of endearment, as of one standing in a special relationship in endearment, because of the nature of that one. In the Hebrew the same word is sometimes translated, *"darling"* and is occasionally applied to Christ: *"I will not leave my darling in Sheol."*. The Lord Jesus, whom the Father sent into the world, is named under a term of endearment in John 3:16. The whole force of that verse centers in the fact that the love of God is there seen in uttermost sacrifice as He takes the final step of sending Christ.

It is not that God was not in a position to beget multitudes of sons, or that God had simply confined Himself to begetting one. The term is used because of what the Son was. God has never begotten another like Him. . .and has never intended to do so. Christ is unique in His relationship with the Father. He stands alone. The Father summed all things up in Him. . .the Father never intended to put anything of Himself in another as belonging to or inherently in that other. If we ever receive of God's fulness it will be only in Christ, not in ourselves. Everything is bound up with Christ. In that way He is unique. He stands alone in the fulness and finality of God. All things are sealed with Him.

This touches upon the crucial nature of the Fall. In Adam we have one whom God created, and the first Adam was called the son of God (Luke 3:38). He was not the son of God in the same sense as Christ, but as being God's offspring, as being one into whom God had breathed the breath of lives. Here was Adam's sin: While he was conditioned by a dependent relationship, and was to have all things as in God by filial fear, obedience and love. . .he yielded to the temptation to take things out of that relationship and have them in himself. Here is how the temptation was presented to him: *"You shall be as God! What you now have only by dependence and obedience, you can have as your own right, prerogative and possession!"* That led to the Fall. From that time forward, God never places in another that which is of Himself to belong to that other as a part of his own being. . .but He has placed all that belongs to Him in Christ and, as it were, locked it up. Now, no one can have anything except in Christ. **"God hath given unto us eternal life,** *and this life is in His Son. He that hath the Son hath the life."* This could be enlarged upon so much more, but suffice that for the time being. Let us leave it here for now: **CHRIST IS THE ONLY BEGOTTEN, THE UNIQUELY BEGOTTEN, THE SINGULARLY BEGOTTEN SON OF GOD!**

It is just there that things have gone astray, and the false teaching has come in to the effect that we are all sons as Christ was a son . . .and that the result of the process of things in us will be our deification. **That has been the Devil's lie from the beginning!** There will be no sonship in us in exactly the same way as that in which Christ is the only begotten. He stands alone!

Having said that general word about the two titles of Christ relative to His Sonship, and repeating that the two titles are Divine, I want to summarize the subject in a few definite points.

Strength and Character Derived from Sonship

(FD 290-29)

First there was a strength and dignity derived by the Lord Jesus from this relationship. You cannot fail to see this as you read the account of His life here on earth. From His relationship with His Father, of which He was quite aware. . .the relationship of Son to Father and Father to Son, He derived a wonderful strength and dignity. This relationship was a secret which others neither knew or recognized. They would not tolerate His claim to this relationship, and even sought to slay Him when He made reference to it. But to Him. . .that He was the Son and that God was His Father meant everything at all times. To break that down somewhat. . .The devil's aim was to bring the Lord Jesus into the realm of questioning, and to coerce or persuade Him into putting that relationship to the test. To have given in to that would have been to have entertained doubt of all that was certain and sure, and to have acted presumptuously, and to have gone back upon an absolute surrender. The Devil's objective was to get Him on the ground of demonstrating something which to His own heart was beyond demonstration and needed not to be demonstrated. Satan wanted to lure Him to put this thing to the test to prove it in times of stress. ***"Tempted at all points like as*** *we ..."*, said the Apostle.

You know what temptation like this is. As one who rejoices in the knowledge that God is your Father, you know what it means to you in the best moments of life. But suppose you are hungry, weak, worn out and in direct conflict with the Devil and the powers of darkness while around you there is a sinister atmosphere of evil. For the moment it seems that you are in a wilderness with all the wild beasts. You listen to the suggestions which th enemy makes at such a time. The insinuations about the Father, and your relationship with Him. *"Tempted in all points like as we ..."* But the Lord Jesus did not yield to the suggestion, to the insinuation. He did not yield to the pressure to subject that relationship to any kind of test. He stood on it. He won on the ground of His secret knowledge of it. He restrained His own soul, and refused to allow it to govern Him. He stood in His spirit upon God's fact and won! It become the strength that enabled Him to win. He knew God's fact to be true. . .and He stood on it!

That gave Him a wonderful strength and dignity. Some of His language, if it were the language of an ordinary man, would be considered terrible as He speaks to the leaders of the religious community. He says to these men who occupy executive positions in religious things: *"Ye shall know the truth, and the truth shall make you free" (John 8:32).* Again He says: *"If therefore the Son of shall make you free, ye shall be free indeed ..." (John 8:36).* They immediately rose up and said: *"We were never in bondage to any man ....", "...we are Abraham's seed."* Jesus proceeded to point out how great their bondage was. The dignity of the position! *"If the Son shall make you free ..."*. It puts Him in a higher place than all the rest, and invests Him with a dignity, an ascendency, and a moral supremacy. I simply note that fact, as it is very clear to all who read the Scripture. He rested so much upon the fact that He was the Son of God and then proceeded to draw His daily strength from it.

Standing on that ground means strength. We may gain confirmation of that fact if we again look at the Old Testament for a moment. What tremendous strength, dignity and executive ability came to Nehemiah through his recognition of the fact that God had given him a mandate, and that he was the man appointed by God to do the work. How much this meant to him when his enemies set their many traps for him. They used every means possible to get him out of his God appointed position and frustrate the work. Finally, in the midst of all of their threatenings, someone counseled him to take refuge in the House of God...his reply was: *"... should such a one as I flee?"* Those were not words of personal conceit. They were the words of a man whom God had appointed and commissioned...words of a man who was assured of God's support. In the same way, the Lord Jesus was able to stand His ground because of the Divine relationship which meant He had Divine backing and support.

Oh, how we need some of this assurance today! It is a wonderful thing to know that God has sent you, and that God is with you, and that you are under a Divine mandate...and that you are related to God! This fact should always prove a secret source of strength and dignity.

Status and Mission Connected with Sonship

(FD 290-30)

This is the second thing. Again, notice some of the statements that are made: *"The Father judgeth no man, but he hath committed all judgment to the Son" (John 5:22). "The Father loveth the Son and showeth him all things that himself doeth" (v 20)* What a position! The writer of the letter to the Hebrews uses this phrase: *"Christ as a Son over God's house..."* Sonship carries with it position and Divine vocation. *"Because He is the Son of Man ..."* That was the Lord's own way of expressing and explaining the prerogatives which were put into His hands.

As Son He was related to or connected with a great Divine purpose. This conferred upon Him the dignity of being related in Sonship to what God had determined from everlasting. He was in that. There is much strength to be derived from the relationship, from the fact that you are connected with some great thing which is of universal, eternal value and significance. This is what sets you apart in your relationship with God. If only the Lord's people would realize that they are not just saved for saving's sake, but in order that by that initial step they should come into a place of tremendous value and importance in connection with an eternal purpose of God

. . .how much it would mean.

Your particular place of ministry may seem small and insignificant (to you), but it is a part of a whole and as such deems it important and valuable to the Kingdom of God and to your Lord. The smallest place is of tremendous significance if it is part of a whole, and the whole can never be a whole without its parts. In the case of the Lord Jesus Christ, of course, the entire purpose was resting upon Him, and He knew it. There was a secret strength derived from what He was here, from that with which He was related. . .the position into which He was brought by the Father. The **third** thing is this:

Ultimate Issues Inherent in Sonship

Have you noticed how this takes you into the distant future? At no time did Jesus ever imply that after a certain period He would finish His work and that for Him it would be the end or He would be finished. He never implied that He would go the way of all flesh, that His work would be done, and His life would be over. Even though He knew the Cross lay in His path, you constantly find Him speaking of things that lay in the future. Crucifixion, death, burial. . .all this might be, yet with great meaning and connection His gaze is seen to be fixed on things that were in the far distant future. After all, the Cross with all of its meaning and significance was an incident. That will pass and the work will go on. A work has been started, and the Cross will not interrupt it. It is an essential incident and an indispensable factor along the way. . .it is something that will be passed through, and the work will be consummated and the end realized.

It was Sonship that gave Him that assurance of the ultimate issue of everything. Will He suffer? Yes, He knows He will suffer. He will be delivered into the hands of wicked men and be crucified. He knows it, and He tells His disciples about it. Will He die and be buried? Yes, He knows it to be a fact. **But with it, all the issues are certain!** They are secured and they are tremendous! Nothing, neither men nor devils, independently or combined, can frustrate the ends. Nothing can curtail the work or prevent the issues. This Sonship is not merely a thing of this earth. It is not something which is but for a time in its relationship and values. This Sonship is eternal. It is abiding in all of its meaning and intention. The issues are secured by the nature of Sonship. Sonship is an indestructible thing. Other relationships might cease, but not this one. The relationship is not something in itself, but something with a mighty universal purpose. He has a marvelous assurance springing secretly out of this Sonship with regard to the issue of everything.

The Lord foretells that He will be delivered into the hands of wicked men, who will crucify Him. But He does not stop there. He goes on to say that the third day He will rise again. **That is Sonship!** You cannot keep Sonship in the grave. Though Sonship will go down into the grave a thousand times, it will not stay there! If the sons of God are crucified ten thousand times they will rise again. Sonship is certain of survival, whatever men and demons do. It gives the assurance that in the end we shall stand triumphant. It carries all the issues with it.

It is an uplifting thing to see Christ as He is presented at the beginning of the book of the Revelation. *"I am the Living One!"* **That is triumph!** *"I became dead ..."*; not, they killed me! *"I became dead ..."*. That is a prerogative of Sonship. *"No man taketh it from me, I lay it down myself." "I have authority to lay it down, and I have authority to take it again" (John 10:18). "This commandment received I from my Father."* There is no triumph of men or devils about that. *"I am the Living One." "I became dead." "Behold I am alive unto the ages of the ages and have the keys of death ..."* He knew it would be so! Sonship secured that. The assurance of the ultimate issue inherent in Sonship carried Him, with a certainty, on through everything into the undying eternity.

The Father's Fulness Included in Sonship

That has been said already. *"The Father put <u>all things</u> into His hands."* Paul gives us a wonderful unveiling of the *"all things"*. Take that phrase in Paul's letters only, and see where it leads. All is in Christ. In Him all Divine fulness dwells. *"The Father hath committed all things unto the Son."* The Father's fulness is included in Sonship.

The Believer and Sonship

I want to briefly consider the matter of our connection with all that has been said. These things which were true in the case of Christ are made available to us in the resurrection-union. . .in the resurrection life. We understand quite well that to be begotten of God is the very first step in a true relationship with Him. *"Blessed be the God and Father of our Lord Jesus Christ who hath begotten us again unto a living hope by the resurrection of Jesus Christ from the dead" (1 Peter 1:3).* Though not in the same way as that in which Christ is the Son, yet in resurrection God has given us the Spirit of His Son, which is the Spirit of Sonship. By sharing His risen life we are brought in a related way into all that is true of Christ. *"Born of the Spirit". . ."Born from above". . ."Which were born of God".* . .such are the designations of the Scriptures. We are related on resurrection ground.

Where that is true, *"the Spirit beareth witness with our spirit that we are the children of God ..."*. What should that result in? — As in the case of the Lord Jesus Christ, it should result in strength and dignity arising out of the inner witness of the Spirit that we are children of God. I don't think we spend enough time dwelling upon what this means. . .upon the reality of that relationship. If we occasionally remind ourselves that we are not just Christians, not just believers in the Lord Jesus Christ, not just adherents to the Christian faith. . .but children of God, possessing His own life by resurrection union with His Son. We should derive strength and dignity from that. This should bring a sense of moral pride to us. We should be spiritually lifted.

Our union with Christ also means that the position and vocation of Christ is to be shared by us, and that the purpose with which He is related and which is bound up with Him as the Son, is the purpose into which we are called. Please understand that whenever you read of **predestination** it is always in connection with sonship . . .not with salvation. Sonship occasioned predestination. God never predestinated some to be saved and others not to be saved. God predestinated unto Sonship. That is something more than salvation. Salvation brings us into the purpose of God. It brings us into relation with His foreknowledge, His foreordaining and predestinating. Allow me to repeat. . .it is related to an eternal purpose. Vocation and position are bound up with Sonship. A child is one born. . .a son is one adopted on the ground of majority and maturity. We are not elected to childhood, to salvation. We are elected to Sonship, to maturity. It is with reference to that that we have to give diligence to make our election sure and to go on to full growth.

It is possible to miss the full purpose of God, even though we remain saved. You can be a child and yet never come to the position and maturity of a son. Position and vocation are connected with Sonship. . .that is, proceeding to full growth. We are called according to His purpose. We are in union with Christ, related to this tremendous vocation of the Son of God through all the ages to be. We are chosen in union with Him to occupy a tremendously high position.

Is it necessary to apply what was said about assurance as to the ultimate issues? We ought to derive secret strength from this. If I were a bond-slave, the position would be so different. But being a son how certain are the issues. We may be pressed down; we may be crushed for a time; we may appear to be overwhelmed; it may seem that men ride over our heads and the enemy gains the advantage for the time being. . .but the fact bound up with our Sonship is that the issues are secured in absolute triumph, and that we shall stand at last in absolute triumph, because of Sonship. If all *"the sons of God"* sang together and shouted for joy in the heavenly realm before this world was (Job38:7), we may be sure that all who are now sons of God will shout and sing for joy when this world is no more. **The sons will!** God will have His sons, despite what the devil may do.

I want you to remember that all this hangs upon resurrection-union. There was a special attestation of Sonship in resurrection. It was typically set forth at the baptism of the Lord Jesus, when on His coming up out of the water heaven was opened, and a voice said: *"This is My beloved Son, in whom I am well pleased ..."*. At the beginning of the Roman letter, Paul tells us that He was set forth as the Son of God by the resurrection from among the dead. A special attestation on the ground of resurrection. And this ground of resurrection is where we come in. The nature of our relationship is that of resurrection-union. The resurrection life of the Lord Himself is the basis of Sonship, and that is why Sonship is indestructible. It is not an official relationship. It is oneness in an incorruptible life . . .in a life that is abiding. It is a wonderful thing to know that

Sonship is based on something that neither earth, nor hell, nor all the antagonisms of this universe can ever destroy though they release their full strength against it.

What have we come into? Not into something that is still open to speculation or chance. We have come into Sonship just at the point where that which is the ground of Sonship, even resurrection life, has triumphed over all the ultimate antagonistic forces of the universe. That becomes the basis of Sonship. What an assurance! What a hope! What a possibility is in resurrection life! What position!

Final Word

Do you have hold of that? That is the tremendous thing about our relationship with God in Christ, that it comes about at the point of His resurrection. How did God bring about the supreme attestation of His Sonship? Satan, with all his myriads. . .with all the power at his command, both spiritual and human. . .was allowed to converge upon Christ. Every evil, deadly, iniquitous force in this universe came against Him. All the power of death came against Him, as did all the power of sin and malice of evil men, to try and cast Him out of His own world. For a while it looked as though they had succeeded. Darkness covered the face of the deep. He is dead and buried. Seemingly, they have triumphed! All the powers of hell are there in their unholy convocation. **THEN GOD INTERVENED! HE RAISED HIM FROM THE DEAD!**

What does that mean? — That there is not a force in this universe that has enough power to bring God's Son to an end. . .to destroy that life! God raised Him from the dead! That means that all those forces have been exhausted. . .and beaten! God raised Him! That is Sonship! That is the nature of Divine Life. It is more than all the combined forces of the universe. *"Declared to be the Son of God with power, according to the spirit of holiness by the resurrection of the dead."*

Then He gives us that life; that tested and tried life; that life which had been subjected to every evil force in this universe. . .and had proved more than them all. That is the basis of Sonship. Do you see the possibilities that are yours in having that life as members of Christ? Do you understand what it means as to position? What it means as to power! What it means as to the eventualities, the issues. What it means as to vocation! This is not just a thing of time. It is not a thing of earth. That life is eternal, universal and infinite. It is that life which is the basis of all. It is that life which makes all possible. I am not speaking of life apart from the Person. ***"God sent forth the Spirit of His Son into our hearts, crying, Abba, Father."*** The Spirit of Sonship!

CHAPTER X

Divine Purpose and Provision

(FD 290-31)

To summarize what has already been said is to say that **"the Lord Jesus had in the background of His life, here among men, various Divine resources, and various secret springs known to Himself alone, upon which He was continually drawing for His life and work."** We might put that this way: *"Christ had His life abidingly in Heaven."*

Though here on earth, He was nevertheless in a spiritual way, and in a very living way. . .in a real and abiding way, in heaven. We are familiar with that particular fragment of His utterances in John 3:13 – *"And no man hath ascended into heaven, but he that descended out of heaven, even the Son of man, which is in heaven."*

From the margin we learn that some ancient authorities omit *"which is in heaven"*. It may be that they are correct in doing so, but it in no way alters the meaning of what the Lord said. If you leave the phrase out you still have a word which carries the force of it: *"No man hath ascended into heaven, but He that descended out of heaven ..."*. Surely if language means anything that means that Christ had an ascended life. If He is drawing a contrast between Himself and all others, the point of contrast clearly lies in this fact of having ascended into heaven or of not having done so. It is the implication of that statement which is so full of meaning. Christ had His life abidingly in heaven.

Our Access to Divine Resources

We have seen Christ as the true spiritual fulfillment of Jacob's ladder, which was set up on the earth, and the top of which reached into heaven. Of this the Lord later said to Nathaniel: *"Hereafter thou shalt see heaven opened, and the angels of God ascending and descending upon the Son of Man."* If the Lord Jesus is the same, in effect, as the ladder of Jacob, then He is both in heaven and on earth. In Him heaven and earth are united. . .are brought together. . .and while He is on earth for purposes of expression and action, He is also in heaven. The point is that **"His life and all of His resources, were drawn from above."** He was in touch with inexhaustible resources. He was in touch with resources which could never die, because they were not of this earth, and which could never be subjected to the touch of corruption which is characteristic of everything on this earth. From time to time He draws contrasts: *"My peace I give unto you. Not as the world giveth, give I unto you ..."*. The contrast lies in the fact that any peace which this world gives is a fading peace; is a perishable peace that does not last. But of the peace that He gives, the Lord Jesus said: *"... not as the world giveth, give I unto you ."*

That which comes from heaven is not subjected to the vanity to which this entire creation is subjected. **Vanity**, as that passage of Scripture makes very clear, simply means **"never coming to completeness or fulfillment, always under limitation and always governed by that which is passing and transient."** That is vanity. The whole creation has been subjected to vanity by an act of God. But Christ does not belong to this creation, nor are His resources from this creation. There is therefore no vanity, no vainness about them.

Because of resurrection that blessed truth may be proved by us also. We notice in First Corinthians fifteen, the exhortation not to faint, not to lose heart, but to be always abounding in the work of the Lord is urged upon us for this reason, namely: *"...forasmuch as ye know that your labor is not in vain in the Lord"*. That great statement is ushered in with a *"wherefore"*, and that word also links us with what has gone before: *". . .death is swallowed up in victory [victoriously]. O death where is thy sting? O grave where is thy victory?" "Thanks be unto God who giveth us the victory*

*through our Lord Jesus Christ" (1 Corinthians 15:54-55, 57).
"Wherefore. . .your labor is not in vain in the Lord ..." (v 58).*
There is no vanity in your labor because it is deathless, for death is swallowed up. On resurrection ground you are brought into touch with the deathless resources of Christ. Those resources were always of an indestructible and endless life. These are our resources in risen-union with Him.

All of that simply means that for our lives and our service, for our ministry and our heavenly vocation, there are resources at our disposal which are heavenly, inexhaustible, and incorruptible. This is the great secret of strength. I have seen something of what those resources are, and of how they operate. I have seen something of their value for spirit, soul and body; of their value to mind, heart and will. **We must remember that He who commissions places His own resources behind His commissioned.** When God guides, God provides. When God leads, God feeds. When God directs, God protects!

An Inescapable Necessity

(FD 290-32)

This simply means that we must abide in heaven as He abode in heaven. That can be expressed in many different words of Scripture. For example: *"walking in the Spirit and not in the flesh; warring after the Spirit and not after the flesh; the weapons of our warfare are not carnal but spiritual."* These are only ways of defining what it means to abide in heaven and not to live as of the earth; to allow no dependence on earthly means, no worldly methods, and never to take ourselves as we are naturally as the final word.

For Christ, in a very real and full way, the heavens ruled in His life. So it must be in our case. The rule of the heavens must decide whether a thing shall be undertaken, and whether or not we can see it to completion. The **visible, what is felt,** and **what appears to our natural eyes** must never be the ground of our decisions. It is a wonderful thing and a tremendous strength to come to the same position as Christ. . .where we know that infinite heavenly resources are available. This is a position to which we gradually come. . .not instantaneously. We only arrive at this place by the road of personal discipline which takes the form of bringing us to utter dependence on the Lord. The result is not an emptying and a breaking down as an end in itself, but one which is accompanied by the grace of God, which, when we are empty, makes His fulness abound.

There is a positive as well as a negative side to this. God does not view negatives as His ultimate goal, but when He breaks and empties us, He does something on the positive side which ever causes us to marvel and, in effect, say: *"That was the Lord and not me."* We progressively come to know by that way of discipline that there are heavenly resources which far outstrip all human possibilities, and that these resources are operative. The Lord leads us so far in making that real and then brings us to a place where we have to take a stand on it. . .lest we begin to take it for granted.

It is possible, and perhaps true of us sometimes, that after an experience of the Lord's goodness in this way, that we sit down in our lazyboy, so to speak, and say, *"He will be gracious like that again. I don't need to bother. I need not worry. The Lord will show us and deliver me again."* We are empty, and cannot of ourselves meet the demand. The Lord must do it! So we become passive. However, He will not pick us up out of our armchair and work through us as robots. He has dealt with us in order to teach us a lesson, and then He calls for a definite exercise of faith in relation to it. So. . .while the truth holds good that **"it is no longer I, but Christ ..."**, that is only half of the statement. We have to remember what follows: **"...the life that I now live in the flesh, I live by the faith of the Son of God ..."** That is the other half of the statement. **"I live... and yet no longer I, but Christ liveth in me."** I live in faith, the faith which is in the Son of God. That is the active side of living by His life. Paul adds this latter half to safeguard the utterance.

Although we may not knowingly fall into the error against which he was guarding, that is, we might not fall into the formulated error, yet we might fall into the error itself. Paul was guarding against pantheism. We have learned that the Greeks were all too open to the pantheistic idea, and they would seize upon that word, **". . .it is no longer I but Christ ..."**, and say, *"Well, it is really a situation of our being merged into the great Divine, and losing our personality, our identity and ourselves in a great All, so that any* *distinctiveness of person or personality is gone."* That is pantheism. These Greeks might have received what Paul was saying in light of pantheism and said, *"Oh, well, that just supports our idea. That just lines up with our concepts."* So Paul immediately protects and rescues his statement from that false conception. ***"I live by faith in the Son of God ..."*** I will retain by own identity. I will retain my own personality. This life of union with Christ is a faith union, not a merging of substance.

While we ourselves might not fall into this error, we might fall into the principle and become more or less passive, thinking it the Lord who will do it all, and that we have little or no place in it. We have a place, and **that place is the definite exercise of faith** in relation to Christ and the heavenly resources. This is what constitutes spirituality. This is what makes a life or a ministry spiritual. It is the drawing upon heavenly resources. It is living the life as out from heaven. That is spirituality. That constitutes a spiritual life and a spiritual walk. The resources are not drawn from self or from the world. . .they are all drawn from above. Everything is so utterly from above, and so utterly not from man, that the life or the work becomes spiritual as a consequence.

There are those who think that spirituality is a kind of **"mystical"** or **"mythical"** something. They think that spirituality is something remote from reality. . .that it is a kind of frame of mind. Spirituality is not a nebulous, mythical, or abstract thing. It is a very practical thing. When men and women are called by God into some facet of Divine ministry, and in the face of demand are conscious that they have no ability or resource to fulfill that ministry. . .when they are conscious that in themselves the thing is utterly impossible . . .and yet when in those circumstances they recognize that they have a living Christ in whom are resources more than enough to meet the demand, and by faith lay hold of Him, and go forward into their ministry with that consciousness — **THAT IS SPIRITUALITY.** And that is tremendously practical. Its very issues prove it to be practical. It is in that way that heavenly things are done. . .and these things cannot be shaken!

Spirituality is not Remoteness

Christ's spirituality **was not** that He was remote from what was practical in everyday life. It **was** that He was bringing heavenly forces and resources to bear upon the practical matters of every day life. You can wash doors, clothes or floors, or do any ordinary domestic things, in spirituality. Many seem to think that spiritual work and ordinary work are two different things. They talk about spiritual work and the "other" work. We must understand that we can bring heavenly resources in to do anything that is legitimate. The doing of those things may be a testimony. The majority of people have no occasion to draw upon heavenly resources for a platform ministry. For the most part, they know how to do it, and most often do it quite well. They just know that the Lord will get them through. Now, exactly the same resources have to come into the ordinary work as into what we call spiritual work. It all has to be done on a spiritual basis, and therefore will be a testimony. We all know that many times just to get through a day's work requires more than ordinary human resources. Spirituality consists in our doing everything as from heaven. We must be careful how we draw a line, lest we make a distinction between the spiritual and the **"rest"**.

Divine Resources for Divine Purpose

(FD 290-33)

Christ never took things for granted. That is to say He never took these heavenly resources for granted. He never allowed the thought that they would just operate mechanically, irrespective of certain conditions on His side. His was a life of exercise in relation to them. Before He chose His disciples, He spent the night in prayer. I think it is correct to say that the two things were in some way related. Of the occasion He later said, *"I know whom I have chosen ..."*. That was said in connection with His having deliberately chosen His betrayer, Judas. To do that demanded Divine government, help and assurance. That also was true of the other eleven. In light of the repeated failure to those men, and especially in light of the final scene before the Cross where they all forsook Him and fled because everything seemed lost. . .did He make a mistake in choosing them?

Is there room for our asking Him: *"Lord, you might have done better if You would have chosen a different group of men. You seemed to have made a mistake in choosing the ones that You did."* Yet He says, *"I know whom I have chosen ..."*

This choosing was governed by a night of prayer. Evidently He found prayer to be a necessity. I don't think we are correct when we assume that to Him prayer was just an opportunity to get away and have a quiet talk with the Father for fellowship's sake. **It was a necessity!** He needed it. Prayer was an avenue for the communication of the heavenly resources. Because of this, His prayer life, rich and strong as it was, makes it perfectly clear that He took nothing for granted as to those resources. We must be careful lest we fall into a snare in this very thing. While these same resources are at our disposal. . .while they are ours in Christ, and while they are intended to be expressed in our lives. . .and while it is true that the sovereignty of God secures them for us, yet these resources will not be ministered to us irrespective of the conditions that exist on our part. We cannot presume upon them. We cannot take them for granted. We cannot neglect prayer. If we do, we will find that they will not function, and that weakness, loss and need will supervene. The Lord Jesus must be our example or pattern in this matter. Well . . .that is a brief summary of the question concerning His resources and ours, when we are joined to Him in resurrection life.

One further word with reference to the fact that all of this lay behind the purpose of His life. There are two things to be said in this connection. One is that **there was a secret strength for Him** which lay in the fact of a Divine purpose. He knew that He was on this earth for a purpose of tremendous significance, and from the fact that He had come for a purpose. . .and that that purpose was connected with His being here. He drew strength for that. The other point is that **these resources were definitely related to the purpose**, and that the strength of those resources would have immediately failed if He at any time moved outside of or away from that purpose. I want to pursue those two things a little more fully. They touch us very deeply in our own experience.

Strength Derived from a Sense of Divine Purpose

As you read the story of His life on earth, you cannot miss the emphatic facts of Divine purpose. Study John's gospel, for example, and underline the many uses of the word *"sent"*. You will first find the word in 4:34. In chapter five you will find it repeated four times. In chapter six, it is again repeated four times. In chapter seven it is repeated four times. In chapter eight, four times. It is used once in chapters nine, thirteen, fourteen, fifteen and sixteen. It is used three times in chapter twelve. Then there is the word *"gave"*, and its cognates, in such passages as 3:16 – *"God so loved the world that he gave ..."* There is purpose in it. *"That"* governs the giving. Trace the use of the word *"come"* through all four Gospels with reference to His advent. *"The Son of Man is come to seek and to save that which was lost ..."*. *"Come"* is related to a purpose. *"I am come that they might have life ..."* Then His use of the word *"works"* provides yet a further instance of this feature. *"I must work the works of Him that sent me while it is day ..." "My Father worketh even until now and I work ..."* He is engaged in something specific and definite. He has come with a purpose. There is a total absence of anything that is of merely incidental value in His life. The immortality of Christ is not to be thought of in mere terms of His doing a work which others would continue to do after His departure. The purpose of His life was clear-cut and unique. He was not here merely to start a movement which was to continue when He was gone and forgotten. He was not here for a campaign or project which others would take up and assume. He was here to do something with which He personally would be associated through all time and eternity. He was here related to a definite and undefeatable purpose.

This is why in the book of the prophet *"Isaiah, He is called the Servant of Jehovah"*. That title meant that He would come to fulfil a purpose of God. He was the Servant of Jehovah, the Servant of a Divine purpose. When you come into the realm of service in His case, you find everything very precise. We are familiar with the outstanding characteristic of Mark's Gospel. It is the Gospel of *"the Servant of the Lord"*. In Mark's writings we immediately see Him — without particulars about His birth or childhood – presented as a

Servant. The language is very precise. Precision characterizes everything in his Gospel. ***"Straightway" [immediately]***, for example, occurs nineteen times. That is the characteristic of a true servant. The Servant of the Lord is here on business. He is not here to play, not here for personal interests or diversion. **He is here with a purpose. . .and to that He is given.** When He summons into relationship with Himself, it is for service - ***". . .and straightway [immediately] they left the nets and went after Him."*** That is business at hand. There is the element of a Divine purpose governing His life. From that consciousness He drew all of His strength.

There is a great deal of strength to be drawn from the realization that things are not incidental or general, but specifically with regard to our being here on this earth; that we are related to an eternal purpose. . .that we are called according to His purpose. Wherever we are, provided we are there after having surrendered our lives to the Lord and have sought His will, we are not to just mark time, or to stand and wait. . .but we are to remember that we are there in relation to a purpose. You would be amazed at how many are just idly putting in time. . .waiting for some great thing to happen. They feel (for whatever reason) that they are in a place where the real purpose of God has no bearing upon their lives. That is a very dangerous mentality spiritually. It may be true that you have not yet come into your ultimate calling, but you are in it relatively now, and will never come into the fulness of it until you are faithful and obedient to all that is before you now. ***"Whatsoever your hand findeth to do, that do with all thy might."*** Your present placement is preparatory to your future ministry. There is something relative to our present position which is tremendously related to God's purpose, and if we see and understand that, we will derive strength from where we are and what we are currently called to do. ***"Where there is no vision the people go to pieces."*** That is but another way of saying that if we fail to have a sense of purpose we lose strength.

Nothing destroys strength more than losing a sense of purpose. Nothing demoralizes more than to lose a sense of a definite purpose. If the enemy can come in and make us feel that we have been mistaken in our calling, in our work, and that we only thought God had called us when in reality He had not. . .then he has destroyed us. We become weak and demoralized and are not able to stand up to anything. **WE ARE CALLED ACCORDING TO HIS PURPOSE!** We need to watch against that pernicious habit of postponing to a **"tomorrow"** which never comes. We must be careful. The devil wants us to waste our lives. Today is the day in which to know the Lord as much as we can, and today's increase in our knowledge of the Lord in its measure is our equipment for a larger ministry tomorrow. The Lord Jesus moved day by day with such assurance and definiteness because He was aware that there was a great purpose bound up with His life, and no day was wasted. *"I must work the works of Him that sent me while it is day ..."* His law of life was day by day to its measure, and every day bound up with the great purpose of God. There is strength in an attitude like that.

In First Chronicles chapter seventeen, we have the Lord's word to David through the prophet with reference to what He was about to do through him and his seed. In verses seven and eight the Lord said: *"I took thee from the sheepcote, from following the sheep, that thou shouldest be prince over my people Israel: And I have been with thee whitersoever thou wentest and have cut off thine enemies from before thee; and I will make thee a name, like unto the name of the great ones that are in the earth."* Additional promises follow: *"I will subdue all thine enemies ..." "... the Lord will build thee an house..." "I will set up thy seed after thee." "I will be his Father." "I will not turn my mercy from him ..."* The Lord has come in with the assurance of a purpose in David's life. He has shown David that a Divine purpose has governed his entire life. He has shown him that He is connected to that purpose and is related to it. As you continue to study, you notice how chapter eighteen is related to chapter seventeen verses one and two. And now David is on his feet with tremendous energy. What has happened? — The sense of Divine purpose marking his life has come to him, and in consequence he is a strong man. All of these enemies existed before, but they were unbroken, undestroyed. Immediately after discovering that his life was no mere casual thing, but that it was bound up with God's sovereign purpose, he becomes a man full of strength to do battle. There is a tremendous strength derived from a sense of Divine purpose in your life. The Lord Himself drew strength from that.

With regard to our union with Christ risen, we have much to

assure us of a purpose as well as the fact that we are connected to it. ***"As the Father hath sent me. . .even so send I you."*** Here again we find the word ***"sent"***. It would take far too long and too much space to present all the evidence we have in Scripture that every one who is **livingly related to the risen Lord** is brought into an eternal purpose though it be by different ways, in different spheres and along different lines. My prayer is that the Lord would bring us to the place where we realize that we are not here just to live our lives in a general sense as Christians, and then die and go to be with the Lord in glory. . .but that we would understand that there is tremendous purpose bound up with it. There is a mystery in

the purpose. We cannot always understand how the Lord achieves His purpose, but somehow He does so in these earthly lives of ours. That is the fact of purpose.

Effectual Service. . .The Fruit of Spiritual Resources

(FD 290-34)

The other thing is that the service was the fruit of spiritual resources. That is to say, it was not **merely** official. It was official; Christ was chosen and appointed for a work. In that sense, He was elected; He held an office, and in it He was fulfilling a special task as appointed or ordained by the Father. His particular work could be done by no one else. But it was not merely official or only official. He did not fulfil it simply because He was One set apart to do that work, and that was all there was to it. Although He was the chosen and appointed Servant of Jehovah, His service was also the result of spiritual resources and not merely by official appointment.

The two go together and must be kept together because one cannot exist without the other. What was official never went beyond the spiritual. It could not. The Lord Jesus could never have fulfilled His purpose, His office without the spiritual resources. It is just at this fact that the disciples, in their ignorance, were in danger. Recall the occasion when the Lord was in the mount and a man brought his child in a very grievous state. The devil had a real foothold in the child's life. The man first brought his child to those disciples who were left at the foot of the mount, and they attempted to cast out the demon. The narrative implies that they made an attempt, and failed. When the Lord came down the man brought the child to Him and said: ***"Master, I have brought unto thee my son, which hath a dumb spirit. . .and I spake to thy disciples that they should cast him out; and they could not."*** Later, when they were alone, the disciples said unto Him, ***"Lord, why could we not cast him out?"*** Evidently they had tried and failed. The Lord says in reply: ***"This kind goeth not out but by prayer and fasting".*** Had they attempted it, then, as officials?

They were disciples. The man had recognized them as Christ's disciples. They were in the official position related to Christ, and so on the official basis they had attempted to do it. . .not recognizing that the **"office"** must be accompanied by the **"spiritual resource"**. No office can be fulfilled even in relation to Christ except on the basis of an accompanying spiritual resource. The **"office"** must not get ahead of the **"spiritual power"**. If it does it will break down. The **"office"** is never a mechanical thing. You may be chosen from before the foundation of the world . . . you may have been ordained from eternity for a special work . . . the sovereignty of God may single you out from the multitudes of earth for a purpose, but you will never fulfil it except on the ground that there is the accompanying spiritual resource. This will not be mechanically, but governed by a relationship from heaven. In the Word of God there is always the difference drawn between vital faculty and vital force.

The Relationship Between Grace and Gifts

Just one or two further points before this chapter closes. I will direct your attention to just two passages of Scripture. ***"But unto each one of us was the <u>grace</u> given <u>according to the</u> measure of the <u>gift</u> of Christ"*** Note the phrase, ***"the gift of Christ"***. ***"When he ascended up on high he led captivity captive, and gave gifts unto men" (Ephesians 4:7)***. The gift of Christ. Grace according to the gift. The we read, ***"and having <u>gifts</u> differing <u>according to the grace</u> that was given to us ..." (Romans 12:6)***.

Grace according to the gift! Gifts according to the grace! Grace given by the gift, that is one side. The other side is the gift given by grace. There is a Divine gift in sovereignty through the members. It may be one of the gifts mentioned in Romans 12, or it may be some other gift for helping or for administration. God has made you a gift to the Church. If He has gifted you to the Church (in office that is) as an apostle, the office is that of an apostle. If as a prophet, the office is that of a prophet. If God has given you to the Church as a gift, you cannot fulfil your office except in so far as the grace comes up to the measure of the gift. Simply put, **the vital force must be according to the vital function.**

However, so often when individuals have thought they were apostles, or evangelists, or prophets, or pastors or teachers, they have viewed the matter in this way: *"I am an evangelist, I am a pastor, I am a teacher. God has made me that. That is my gift."* And they have tried to fulfil their function simply because it was the gift, and they were resting upon the gift rather than upon the grace. It is a very dangerous thing to become an official and not keep the vital force in proportion to the office. That is what has made **"professional clergy"**. To express it again the other way, **the gift is according to the grace.**

How can I best illustrate that truth? — The importance of the matter is that the two things have to be kept together in equal measure. . .gift and grace or gift and function. If you divorce them or place one above the other, there will be a complete nullifying of any fruitful result, or else they will go out of balance and the entire thing will become lopsided. Suppose you build a power plant that generates enough electricity to give light and energy to an entire city. . .and yet you have no wires, lights or switches. What good is it? You have vital force without vital function. You have a tremendous amount of power, but it is unrelated to any need or situation. There is no result. You can also have the opposite case: You have all the needed things. . .wires, lights, switches, etc. . .but no power plant. To accomplish the task, you need both! Also if you overload your wiring and your lights with power you, again, will meet disaster. The gift must be adjusted to the grace . The gift must be according to the grace. If you divorce the two you have nothing at all.

I realize that is a poor illustration, but it may serve to help us a little. We must remember that God's resource is according to the purpose to which He has called us. If we try to stretch ourselves beyond our measure (our gift), the vital force (the Spirit' power) will not be sufficient. If we try to step into something for which God has never chosen us we will lack in resource. If we try to take on something more than the apportioned gift that is particularly ours, it will prove disastrous. It is God who has **appointed, adjusted and arranged** the Body. We can never take it upon ourselves to say what work we shall do for the Lord. History has shown the many disasters that have occurred when individuals have decided for themselves how and where they are going to work for the Lord. It is a terrible thing for a man to try to fulfil a teaching ministry when God has appointed him to be an evangelist. Many will remember William Branham. He was one of the great men of God used to bring the healing power of God to his generation. However, he wanted to be a teacher. Try as he would, he only brought theological confusion to the Body in his attempts at teaching. End result: God took him home. . .the Church lost a great healing ministry! I simply use him as an illustration of the truth being conveyed at this point in our study.

Final Word

If the Lord has called us to a work, then His resources are available right up to the fulness of that calling. The supply is there according to the gift. . .the grace according to the gift. . .the vital force according to the vital function. It is all there! We must be careful that we do not manufacture the calling or the appointing.

That is where our union with the risen Lord is so important. We are to be governed by life, through union with the risen Lord. My point is that these heavenly resources are related to a Divine purpose. The resources will be forthcoming as we enter into the purpose, as we keep within our measure and draw upon them. They are there for the purpose of God. There is strength to be derived from the resources for the purpose, and there is strength to be derived from the fact of the purpose itself.

CHAPTER XI

The Function Of A Resurrected Life

(FD 290-35)

Up to this point in our study, we have been occupied and concerned with personal things. It is vitally important that we should have that side of things put before us first, but we must not stop there. When we have come to the place of our own personal appropriation of the resources which are in Christ for us, then we have to recognize that connected with such appropriation there is a purpose that reaches far beyond ourselves alone. It is at this point that we begin to turn our eyes outward instead of inward, while still occupied with the same supreme matter. . .Christ risen and the eternal Word. So our time of meditation at this juncture is upon **the reproduction of an adequate life in the Church**. . .to its essential and vital expression.

Adam and Eve have often been used as types of Christ and the Church, and perhaps rightly so. The injunction given to them was that they should be fruitful and multiply. That law in a spiritual way is also carried over to the antitype, Christ and the Church. The law of this one life, of this oneness in life into which Christ and His own have been brought, is **fruitfulness. . .increase. . .and reproduction.**

We should remember that **life** is a trust. By it a stewardship is created. **Life** is not something to be received, and, so to speak, pocketed or appropriated just for the good of the recipient. **Life** is a trust with which we are called to trade, and by means of which we are under an obligation to secure increase. **Life** demands a right of way for transmission, and to deny that right of way is to violate **life**, to be disloyal to the greatest of all trusts.

In the history of peoples, Israel stands out as perhaps the most conspicuous example of this law. Israel was chosen to be a representation of great Divine, spiritual laws among all the people of the earth. Consequently, her national life was the embodiment of a spiritual principle. It was the outward representation of something deeper, of something heavenly, of something Divine. In your reading of the Old Testament, you probably have already recognized how in the life of Israel the family had a very large place. . .and the larger the family the happier the people. Not to have a family was a tragedy. If that were not possible, then the whole life was regarded as being blighted or spoiled. That was a ruling fact in Israel.

That fact is one which lies near the surface and, as already has been said, one can hardly fail to recognize it. But as you do so, you will see that in that particular, as in many others which perhaps are more obvious, **there is embodied a spiritual law**. Israel was chosen for the reproduction and propagation of the things of God. The Lord deposited His heavenly things with Israel, not that she should appropriate them and close them up within herself, but should trade with them, and regard them as a stewardship. The oracles were for a stewardship. The Divine blessings were a stewardship entrusted to Israel for the world. The great word to Abraham was that *"all"* the families of the earth should be blessed in his seed. The covenant with Abraham was for the general good and blessing of mankind, and there were the elements of a stewardship deposited with the covenant of promise.

Israel failed in the trust and in doing so sealed her own doom. That is shown by the ***"barren fig tree"***. The Lord Jesus came to the fig tree expecting to find fruit on it, but He found nothing but leaves. That fig tree, as stated above, was a type of Israel. It represented Israel. He cursed the fig tree and it withered away. So, with the close of the earthly life of the Lord Jesus, Israel passes out of the place of Divine stewardship, and has never occupied it since. **"The kingdom of heaven shall be taken away from you and given to a nation bringing forth the fruits thereof."** That is but another way of saying, *"You have failed to bring forth the fruit of that which was offered to you, which was entrusted to you. You have defaulted in the matter of your stewardship. You have been barren when you ought to have been fruitful. You have sealed your own doom."* The doom of an instrumentality is sealed by failure to fulfil the vocation for which it was raised up.

An organism is never an end in itself, and is never something for itself. It is a means to a larger end. . .it is a channel for larger purposes. The object of an organism is to reproduce itself by life. That reproduction is always sacrificial. It always costs. It is always by the vessel's yielding up of itself in some way. That is to say . . .death is always to increase. Reproduction is sacrificial.

That brings us to the passage of Scripture in which the Lord summed up everything with regard to His future relationship with His own, and the result of His having come into this world. The passage is ***John 12:24 - "Except a grain of wheat fall into the earth and die, it abideth by itself alone; but if it die, it beareth much fruit."*** Then ***verse 25*** says: ***"He that loveth his life shall lose it; and he that hateth his life in this world shall keep it unto life eternal."*** That embraces and embodies all that I have been saying. Unless a life propagates it remains without being marked by any purpose. It is an end in itself, and God never meant any organism to be that. It saves it own life by letting it go, that increase may be the result. The **law of increase** is sacrifice — ***"Except a corn of wheat fall into the earth and die ..."*** There is no propagation. . .there is no increase. . .there is no reproduction except by letting all that is merely personal go, in the interest of what is more. This leads us to several things. The first is:

The Character and Essence of Christ Risen as Our Life

(FD 290-36)

Christ risen is shown to be a reality for inward expression and experience. The risen life of the Lord is to be in us. Christ is to be in us by His life and by His Spirit of life. The inward meaning and value of Christ risen is the reproduction of His life in all those in whom He is, that all those who have Him dwelling in them in the power of His risen life should be an expression of Christ in life . . .should manifest Him in the power of that life. It is the reproduction of the Christ life in us. The law of that reproduction in us is that we ourselves should die, should accept the position of death, so that all personal life and personal interest is put away, is shed, is parted with. . .and Christ becomes everything. That is what Paul meant when he said: *"I have been crucified with Christ; yet I live, and yet no longer I, but Christ liveth in me ..." (Galatians 2:20).* Here is the expression of Christ produced because all life which is not of Christ has been yielded to the Cross, has died. It has fallen into the grave of the Lord Jesus, and out of the grave there has come an expression of Him.

In our union with Christ in His death we cease and He begins, and from the beginning He becomes the *"all"*. There is a progressive thing, as well as a basic thing. It is a thing all-inclusive in its meaning and intent, but it is also progressive. We have to accept the fulness of that thing in an act. We have to take the position (definitely and consciously) that now, in accepting our union with Christ in His death, this is to work out in our having no more place at all . . .and that whenever **"we"** come into evidence we shall be smitten, we shall be put aside and not allowed to continue. We have to accept that once for all in a definite act of commitment, that from this moment forward, everything that is of **"self"** is going to be smitten unsparingly with that Cross. We must declare that whenever **"self"** tries to gain entrance it will not be allowed to have a place. We need to settle this matter once and for all. We need to have a meeting with the Lord on that inclusive, comprehensive and utter ground, that He will make His meaning in that real. Not our understanding of it, not our grasp or apprehension of it, not what we think to be the **"I"** which is to be forbidden, but what He knows to be the **"I"**. Not the measure of our knowledge of ourselves, but His knowledge of us. There will be revealed a great deal more that is **"I"**, than we ever imagined. Self, then, not as we know it, but as He knows it through and through, is to be brought under the power of that Cross . . .and this we accept in an act.

Then it becomes progressive. To die daily, to be always bearing about in the body the dying or the deadness of the Lord Jesus, so that His death is a working thing every day by which self is denied, is the issue of our initial acceptance. But as that takes place — the sacrificial yielding to the Cross — the life of Christ is being reproduced. By the power of His own life He is increasing while we decrease.

We shall never meet a challenge to set ourselves aside but what, in meeting that challenge, and answering to it, there will be the occasion for an increase of Christ. Everything which demands that we accept a fresh measure of the meaning of His death means that, as we accept it, there will be a larger measure of Him in risen life.

So we can see and understand more fully that the meaning and value of Christ risen as an inward life is **reproduction**. There is no other way. According to the New Testament, that is the only way men and women can become Christians. The increase of the number of the Lord's own is not by joining something from the outside. . .it is by coming to the Cross and dying (an inner work!). There is no Christian on any other ground than that he died with Christ and has been raised together with Him.

The Necessity of Everything Being of a Living Character

This is the second thing. It takes us back to the initial things that were shared in this study about it being contrary to the mind of God to systematize Christianity, Christian truth or Christian order, and appropriate it or apply it as a system. **It must be the issue and outcome of life.** Reproduction is only by life. It is not by truth as a system of doctrine. Reproduction is not by the setting up of some Christian order. It is by life. And herein is the necessity for **everything to be of a living character.** If Christ is to be multiplied, using that word in the right sense — I trust no one will think that I mean that there will be a multiplication of Christs in the literal sense — it can only be through everything being living and of a vital order. This brings us to the third thing, which will, to some extent, elucidate and explain what was just said.

The Nature of the Church

(FD 290-37)

First, **the constitution**. What is it that constitutes the Church? — We now know that the Church is not constituted upon the Christian creed; nor upon a set of beliefs; nor by assent to certain doctrinal propositions. The Church is not constituted by asking people to join it, become members of it or adherents to it. . .the Church is constituted by the transmission of the risen life of the Lord Jesus Christ. **Reproduction is its law of increase.**

Increase may be brought about in two ways. **One is the way of imitation**. You can turn out so many things by making them on a pattern, and thus increase by imitation. It hardly needs saying that this **is not** the New Testament way of reproduction. **The other way is by conception**, that is, by the out-growth of life from within . . .the form which life takes when it expresses itself. It is internal rather than external. The difference between imitation and what is conceived is the difference between what is dead and what is alive. One is made . . . the other is born. The constitution of the Church is the result of the activity and energy of the life of the risen Lord being transmitted, being passed on. Whatever you may develop, you will never get a development of **the true Church** unless the life of the risen Lord is operative and is there in sufficient measure to be transmitted by the Spirit.

Second is **the Order**. The same law holds good as to the order of the Church. It is the result of His life. Again, two kinds of things are possible. You can **appoint to office**, and set apart with certain titles and names, which represent certain spheres of activity or kinds of work and responsibility. You can elect or vote into such office or position, and proceed along that line, setting up the Church order. Or you can follow another line and **be ruled by the law of life**. In this course, notice is taken of the working and expression of the Lord's life in the members of the Church. Observation is made of the way in which the members, by that life, begin to show characteristics of certain spiritual ability. Ability is manifesting itself in this way or that way, and in due course, by a spontaneous expression, and by the result of the life of the Lord having its own way in them. . .the Church is compelled to take notice of the fact that "such-and-such" in its midst are spiritually qualified. And as spiritually qualified, they are already, by the operation of this Divine life, the right person or persons for "such-and-such" ministry. That expression of life may manifest itself in a ministry of teaching or a ministry of administration . . . or a variety of other gifts and callings. It is not just natural ability. It is not the result of natural advantages, or training or preferential opportunities. There is the spiritual characteristic about it. Then the Lord's people take notice of it and say, *"It is very evident that the Lord has gifted so-and-so in this certain area. We must do all within our power to allow it to have its full expression."* And so the Church comes into New Testament order along the line of **LIFE**.

A question may present itself to us in connection with the familiar phrases in Ephesians: ***"He gave some apostles; and some prophets; and some evangelists; and some pastors and teachers; for the perfecting of the saints unto the work of ministering ..."*** **When the Lord did that, did He announce to the Church what He had done**? Did He say, *"Now, I have definitely given into your midst so-and-so as your apostle, and so-and-so as your prophet, and so-and-so as your evangelist, and so-and-so as your pastor and teacher?"* Or was His gift secret, only manifesting itself as they went on with Him, and it became noticed that they were developing in certain areas of ministry. (I only pose that as a question for thought!) I honestly think that is how it generally was. As the fruit of obedience the perpetuation of His heavenly order was not mechanical, official or ecclesiastical, but vital, living and spiritual. True order is the expression of life.

That is tremendously important. The Lord does not leave it into our hands to appoint our ministers. . .He does not leave the task of making either the ministry or the minister to us. The Lord develops ministry by **LIFE**, and where the Lord develops ministry, the Church has to take notice. It may be perfectly true that the appointment has been made by God, but it may be equally true that it has to be made manifest by **LIFE** before it comes to function. I believe that is why Barnabas and Paul were detained at Antioch so long. Paul was definitely called and chosen. There was no doubt whatever that heaven had ordained him as an apostle, and all the signs of an apostle were in him. Yet, with the sovereign choice, and with the personal commission to go, he first had to go into Damascus to be told what he should do as one in the church, the assembly, and subsequently he had to tarry at Antioch as a member of the church there for over a year. Even then the Lord did not come to Saul or to Barnabas, his companion, and say, *"Now go out to the work to which you know I have called you."* The Lord gave direction through the leading elders of the assembly: *"Separate unto me Barnabas and Saul for the work whereunto I have called them."* And the church was able to do that, not simply on the basis of a command, but because it had been proved in their own midst that these men were called for this ministry. They had revealed in their local church by **LIFE** that they were called to a ministry. That is the way by which the Lord reveals His ministers.

That brings us to this point: **You do not know what your ministry is unless you daily go on with the Lord.** You may have been Divinely ordained and sovereignly chosen. There may be a great potential for valuable ministry evident in your life. You may not even know anything about it yet. . .and yet it may be perfectly true that the Lord could say that you are a chosen vessel unto Him. But you will only discover what your ministry is as you go on with the Lord in life. As His life increases in you, and your communion with Him goes on unhindered in all of its meaning and value . . . then you will discover that the Lord is moving in you in a certain direction, and that you are becoming stirred or drawn to a certain ministry. None of us really discerns His ministry by being told before hand. We only know it as we go on with God, and His life has its way in us.

That is an important thing because ministry hangs or fall upon life. It does not rest upon mechanical appointment. We cannot make ministers. It is only the risen Christ who can make ministers, and He makes them in the power of His risen life. Only disaster lies before the one who tries to be a minister without the risen life of Christ. The Lord deliver us from ever trying to be ministers without its being the result of His life in us. The life of the risen Lord takes its own form, expresses itself in its own way, and always according to the mind of Him whose life it is.

The Growth of the Church

I have already touched upon this, but I feel a need to repeat and re-emphasize that the growth of the Church is on **the principle of LIFE**. We can never go into all the world gathering people together, asking them to accept certain things which we say about Christ, and then forming them into churches. The Lord has not called us to

"form churches". That is not our business. Would to God that men had recognized that fact. A very different situation would exist today from that which does exist, if that had been recognized. It is the Lord who expands His Church, and it is the Lord who governs its growth.

Our task is to live in the place of His appointment in the power of His resurrection. If, in the midst of others, the Lord can get but two of His children, in whom His life is full and free, to live on the basis of that life . . . and not to seek to gather others to themselves or to get them to congregate together on the basis of their acceptance of certain truths or teaching. . .but to simply witness to what Christ means and is to them, He then has an open door to reach all men. As witness is simply and livingly borne in this way, many will eventually be provoked to say: *"I wish I had what they have!"* And others will say: *"I really covet his experience. That is exactly what I have been looking for!"* Individuals like these will either come to enquire about the way of salvation, or opportunity will be found to lead them to the Lord. **It is in this way that the Church grows.**

I realize that its growth may be furthered at a street corner as you preach Christ and someone responds, and believing on Christ with the heart and confessing Him with the mouth, life is given by the Spirit and they become the Lord's. But the Church is not increased by simply going and getting a building and trying to get people to come to it, and then forming them into a local church. That is not the way. Growth is by life, and this, to begin with, may be by the entering into life of but one soul, and then of another and another. Or it may even be more rapid. But the point is that it is increase because of **LIFE**. That is the growth of the Church. For the growth of His Church, the Lord must have life channels, life centers. Then sooner or later one of two things will happen. It will be abundantly manifest that Christ is fully and finally rejected there, or else there will be an adding, a growth. There is tremendous power in life. . .and the life of the Lord either kills or quickens. It all depends on the attitude taken toward it. He is a savor of life unto life, or of death unto death. Things can never remain neutral. What the Lord really needs is a host of life centers around the world.

Final Word

The irreducible minimum, and yet the adequate means, to begin with, is two; two who are one in His life and two in whom there is co-operation in that life. He sent them forth two by two. That is the nucleus of the Church. It is those that the enemy will seek to separate, quench or kill. He wants to destroy them spiritually, so far as their value to the Lord is concerned for propagation. The Lord's advantage is connected with the fellowship of two in the one life.

We can now begin to see why in the main issue it is so important that all the resources of the risen Lord should be utilized by us . . .should be lived by us. His fulness should become the basis of our lives. Their purpose does not end with us, nor is it something for us, and if we turn them to that end we will die. That provision is for the Lord's end. . .which is **REPRODUCTION**. . .the reproduction of His risen life.

CHAPTER XII

The Law of Permanence

Scripture Lesson: 2 Kings 7:1-2, 16-20; Luke 1:5, 8-15, 18-23; Romans 12:1-2

(FD 290-38)

As we draw this study about the risen Lord and the eternal Word to a close, we want to look to Him for that which will bring all that He has said to us at this time to some point of practical conclusion.

The passages have suggested what the issue is. Their message lies on the surface, so that we do not have to seek deeply for it. They quite clearly, I believe, say to us that although the Lord has His own wonderful and boundless resources, they are resources beyond us and altogether outside of our realm of natural apprehension and understanding. . .yet they are nevertheless at our disposal, and for us in Christ Jesus. However, when everything has been said that can be said as to the fact and nature of these resources, and of our necessity for them, they still remain in Him, and are not of practical value in our own experience until we exercise appropriating faith in relation to them. **The link between His fulness and our need is FAITH.**

The two passages which are before us from the book of **Kings** and the **Gospel of Luke** are striking examples of a loss, through not exercising faith in God in relation to what was humanly impossible. In one case this loss was even unto death, and in the other case it was unto a silenced ministry. In both cases a **miracle** was required. In both cases what was foretold was totally outside of the realm of the ordinary operation of nature. In both cases the Lord said that what had been foretold could be, and should be. But in both cases there were those who were very closely connected with the Lord's things who questioned, who doubted, who allowed nature to govern and dominate. Because of the tremendous difficulty in the way — not an imaginary difficulty, but a real one — because of the condition of things or character of the situation, they took nature as the criterion rather than God's assurance, God's promise and God's word.

The man in the story in 2 Kings 7 lost his life, while Zechariah, for a time at least, lost his ministry. These two things may be interpreted spiritually. Our spiritual life will certainly be forfeited by unbelief. This life in Christ, this risen life of the Lord, will only be known, enjoyed and expressed, as we by faith, transcend the natural conditions and believe in God more than we believe in the situation. Ministry can also be curtailed and limited for the same reason. There may come into our lives an experience which corresponds to Zechariah's being mute for a season; that is, that on certain things of tremendous importance we have no testimony; we are silent; there is a suspending of the fuller values of ministry.

The passage in Luke also presents us with a contrast. When the message came to Zechariah's wife, there was anything but silence in her case. She burst into a great song. We have that beautiful song of worship on record. But Zechariah is mute and silent.

The Nature of True Worship

These things are parabolic, and they lead us to this passage in Romans 12. *"I beseech you therefore brethren, by the mercies of God, to present your bodies a living sacrifice, holy, acceptable to God, which is your reasonable service (your spiritual worship)."* That is the first stop. These words present a picture of the priest taking the unresisting sacrifice in his hands to the altar, where without any rebellion he is able to take its life, and offer it a burnt offering unto the Lord. *"Present your bodies a living sacrifice"*, unresisting, un-rebelling, unquestioning. **Worship is giving God His place and His rights.** Spiritual worship implies that we do not put any questions of ours in the place of God's will.

Then, as though he would explain that in spiritual terms, the Apostle says, *"and be not fashioned according to this world: but be ye transformed by the renewing of your mind ...".* Is that not a beautiful exposition of these other passages which I have mentioned? What does it mean to be conformed to the world? — We know that the governing principles of this world are the **principles of sight and reason**, of argument according to what is called common sense. The world is always saying that *"you must take things as you find them; you must recognize facts, and the facts are these. . .the situation is this, and it is perfect folly to shut your eyes to it; you must take facts into account and reckon with them."* And for this world, the facts have always been the things which are seen, the things as they exist. The world thinks it is utterly absurd to say that what exists is not to be taken as the final argument. That is the world.

The Lord Jesus never asks us to make facts other than what they are. He never says to us, *"these things are not what they are"*, and that we should try my some mental process of imagination to make things other than they are. But He does call on us to see that there is something greater or higher than things as they are. Faith goes beyond this world's facts. The world calls them **"the hard facts"**, but faith can dissolve hard facts. To be conformed to this world is to say, like the man on whom the king leaned, *"**The fact is that we are starving! Everything in the city has been devoured for food, except for a few horses that are left, and we are perishing in the severity of the siege. That is the fact, that is the situation! To say that the entire position can be reversed by this time tomorrow, and that in 24 hours we shall not only be getting something to eat, but getting it at an absurdly low price, even if God were to make windows in heaven that would be doubtful!"*** That is conformity to this world.

It was the same in the case of Zechariah. In the presence of the angel, he said, in effect, **"Well, the facts are that I am an old man, and my wife is an old woman; we cannot be blind to this fact. Nothing can alter the facts."** That is conformity to this world. That is how the world reasons.

The Apostle Paul says: **"Be not conformed to this world ..."** Do you notice how he applies this to the mind? **". . .but be ye transformed by the renewing of your mind ..."** That may well be comprehensive and touch it all. It may touch our manner of life. It may touch everything that we would call worldliness in every direction whatsoever. But here is the special application to our present purpose: **A renewed mind changes the outlook, changes the attitude, changes the consciousness, changes possibilities and therefore changes the individual in whom the mind is renewed!**

Bringing that fact to bear upon the incidents in the passages before us, as well as all other similar situations, that word simply means that we must have another mind about things. . .we must have a new mind. . .not the mind of the world, not the natural mind. The mind of the Spirit says: *"Well, the facts are these; the situation is a very difficult one; nature most definitely declares the position to be one of utter impossibility, but the Lord has given an assurance, a promise, an unveiling of possibilities; The Lord has said that there are resources which are beyond the reach and range of nature, and faith, bridging the gap, represents another mind. . .a renewed mind.* Then you **"may prove what is that good, and acceptable, and perfect will of God."** Then you are like the living sacrifice, not dwelling on the nature side where the old Adam holds control, but on the spirit side, where God is your criterion, your argument. All of that means that we are challenged in relation to the resources of Christ. In the presence of any given need or demand, for which provision has been made in Christ, we are called upon to take the attitude of appropriating faith.

I can see how this entire study, wonderful as may have been the truths stated, the Divine provision unveiled, and the glorious possibilities mentioned, but inevitably lead to that. Is it to be like that? – That is for us to decide. Are we going to take our stand upon this ground, and in faith, as necessity arises. . .as occasion presents itself. . .as demands come upon us, stand there and exercise faith by which the Lord can make it good in us? It is only in this way that the permanent value of anything is entered into. The supreme importance of that which is permanent and abiding is one of the many things upon which emphasis has been laid in this study.

The Law of Permanence in Relation to the World

If there is one thing that is clear about the Word of God and the New Testament in particular, it is that it regards this world in its present state, along with all that has to do with it, as of transient duration. . .simply put, as being a passing thing. It is regarded as in a state of transience. ***"The world passeth away and the fashion thereof."*** Men are deceived by their own reasoning into thinking that because they are achieving so much more, and making the world so much better by all of their technology and advancements, that in a matter of time this world will become a Utopia. The truth is that man is only discovering and now using what already exists. God takes the attitude that all that man discovers and brings to the world has already existed. In effect, He says: *"I made that! That was already there! You have only now discovered it. Before you were created, I was already here and made all that is made. You spend your entire life discovering things, and then you are gone, but have not added one thing to the content of the universe by all your discovery."*

So, because of this transient, passing nature of things, the whole emphasis of the New Testament is upon the heavenly order, heavenly relationship, heavenly resources and the fact that the believer is completely separated from this world in every way as his life and his sustenance, and is a heavenly being with everything heavenly. Though he be here on earth, he is living as from heaven. That makes for permanence, and that is what gives permanence to the believer's life. It is that which is summed up in the risen Lord, and in His risen life. It is the life which is permanent, and which is not of this world. Personal union with the risen Lord and His resources makes for the eternal character of the believer.

The Law of Permanence in Relation to the Church

The same principle applies to the heavenly and spiritual nature of the Church. When this study was begun, it was given the title of, **"The Risen Lord and the Eternal Word"**. It was that element of permanence which was in my heart in relation to our union with the Christ risen. The Church is something which is permanent, which cannot be shaken. . .because it is united with the risen Lord. It is the visible expression of the risen Christ, and everything called the Church which is other than that will pass away.

That is the entire message of the letter to the Hebrews. ***"Yet***

once more I shake not the earth only, but also heaven." The things which can be shaken will be shaken, and the things which cannot be shaken will remain. An immediate application to the whole Jewish system was then in view. The letter was written about the time when Jerusalem was to be hurled to the ground, and its temple left with not one stone upon another. . .and the Jewish believers, being tempted to return to Judaism, were being warned by this letter that the time was at hand when there would be such a shaking of all things of this earth, even religious things. . .that everything that was attached to this earth would be shaken to its foundation and brought down and then pass away.

The only hope for believers was that they should be part of something heavenly, something spiritual that would never be shaken or pass away. The heavenly nature of the Church was revealed in contrast to the earthly nature of Judaism. The permanent nature of the Church in contrast to the transient, temporal nature of the Jewish Church. The true Church is eternal, because it is heavenly, and only on the grounds of heavenliness is it possible for the gates of Hades to be defeated, and for the Church to triumph.

Spiritual Gifts and Ministry

I cannot close this study without applying these same **principles of permanence** to the many elements of gifts and ministries in the Church. They have been previously touched upon, however, I want to mention them again to show the connection of this permanent element or the abiding elements in Spirit given gifts and ministry. To show this, we must return to those portions of the New Testament where ministry and spiritual gifts are mentioned. If you go over the lists as are found in First Corinthians and Romans, you will notice the Apostle uses this law of permanence as a means to determine the value of the gifts. In One Corinthians twelve, Paul goes through the gifts and catalogues them. He then brings the rule of permanence to bear upon them all, and in the following chapter goes on to say that the time will come when many of them will pass away.

Those who are not proponents of the present day ministry of the Holy Spirit will argue that that day has come, and so the many manifestations [gifts] of the Holy Spirit no longer exist. Some even go so far as to say that those who allow the Spirit to manifest the several gifts listed in Scripture are doing so by the power of the devil and the power of God. Those are very dangerous statements and one should be very careful in making them. Those gifts that are most often attacked today are **"tongues", "interpretation of tongues" and "prophecy"**. I have been in the work of God for more than forty years, and if I have learned anything about the Lord it is that He is still moving today in ways that, at times, are totally misunderstood my many. God is actively involved in the current work of the Church. . .in fact, if He ceased to be involved, the work would cease.

I have experienced all of the many gifts listed in these passages and know from personal experience that the Lord has not ceased to express or manifest Himself through the Holy Spirit. The truth is, He continues today more than ever, because the time is short, the task is not complete, and the workers are incapable in themselves to accomplish what must be done quickly. We are told in the Scripture that when one speaks in tongues, he is not speaking to men, but to God. All speaking to God (in whatever form used) is prayer. So, the great wisdom of God allows men and women to speak to Him in a language "unknown" to man. This is done for several reasons. **First**, there are times when we must speak to God so that the enemy cannot intercept our conversation. He must not know what we are asking God to do or are asking Him for. If he knew, he would set out to hinder or attempt to thwart the answer from coming. We see this very clearly in the book of Daniel. His prayer (in his known language) was heard the very first day, yet it took twenty-one days for the answer to arrive because Satan intercepted the delivery and entered into heavenly warfare. He knew what Daniel was praying for. Had he been able to pray in tongues, the petition would have gotten through and the answer delivered without any warfare . . .because the enemy would not have known what was happening. This is just one reason why tongues is a valid and valued gift today.

A **second reason for tongues** is that many times we do not know what to pray for as we ought, so the Holy Spirit prays through us (in tongues) bringing petitions to the heavenly throne so that specific needs might be met or specific situations might be addressed. In recent months the Lord has brought me to another level of prayer and ministry. He is bringing me to the nations.

However, there are times when the burden of the nations grips my spirit and still I do not know how or what to ask the Father to do. It is in those moments that the Holy Spirit takes over and begins to lift the needs to the Father. I am aware of a release and a lifting of that particular burden after this has taken place. I understand that there are many reading these words who may not understand what I am saying. Ask God to teach you about the present ministry of the Holy Spirit. A simple word of caution: **DON'T ALLOW SATAN TO CAUSE YOU TO RIDICULE OR MAKE LIGHT OF THE HOLY SPIRIT AND HIS PRESENT WORK IN THE WORLD, THE CHURCH OR THE LIVES OF THOSE WHO HAVE SURRENDERED THEMSELVES TO HIM.**

Final Word to the Study

I think this is enough for the moment. However, we must be initiated into the secrets of the Lord, and that process comes by way of the Cross. The work of the Cross is a daily process whereby we experience death to all that desires only that which is temporal and earthly. He wants us to become desirous of what is spiritual and permanent. The bottom line to all that I have attempted to communicate through this study is that we must be baptized into Christ and receive the gift of the Holy Spirit. It is all a matter of knowing the Lord in the power of the Holy Spirit, and being delivered from everything that has even the slightest hint of that worldliness which all to often is only thought of in such limited terms, as of its being worldly if you go to certain places or do certain things. It may be that too, but worldliness is something far deeper than that. **Worldliness is bringing the world's standards and values to bear upon the things of the Spirit.**

There was much worldliness in the church in Corinth. They loved tongues, healings and miracles, yet they only allowed those manifestations to bring satisfaction to their flesh. That is why they were passing away in their lives and corporate ministry. There was no permanent value being evidenced. So the Apostle brought the permanent to bear upon everything, and in effect he said, *"the thing which contributes to the largest amount of permanent spiritual value is to be the thing for which we have concern."* So of all these wonderful gifts he says that they are, in the Lord's mind, for edifying — the Greek word is ***"buiding up"*** — and when they are not allowed to build up, they go out of their orbit and cease to fulfil the purpose of the Lord. That is why gifts and manifestations of the Holy Spirit are not found in most churches today.

I have touched upon these things in this broad way to emphasize one principle: **the value of things is to be judged by their spiritual permanence, and the measure in which they lead to spiritual**

maturity. That is only another way of saying, "away from the earthly and to the heavenly. . .away from the temporal and to the eternal. . .away from self and to the Christ! May He be praised for all eternity.

Printed in the United States
20848LVS00007B/106-177